KaAbBa: The Great Pyramid is The Tree of Life: MerKaBa

Secrets Revealed in The MerAkhutu

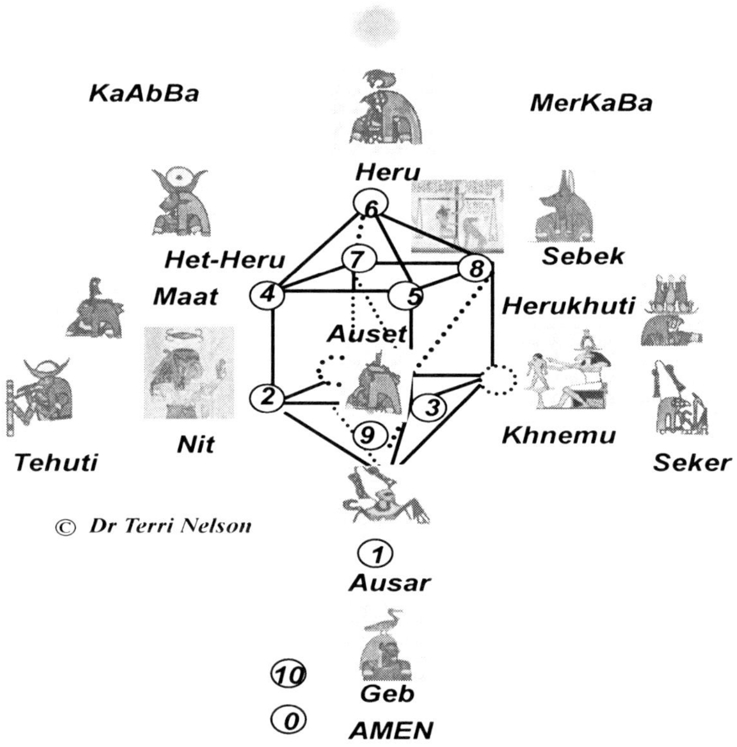
KaAbBa
MerKaBa
Heru
6
Het-Heru
7
8
Sebek
Maat
4
5
Herukhuti
Auset
2
3
9
Nit
Tehuti
Khnemu
Seker
© Dr Terri Nelson
1
Ausar
10
Geb
0
AMEN

Paut Neteru, Solar Bark, Chariot of the Gods

D1548045

Dr. Terri Nelson/Nteri Renenet Elson

The Neteru revealing Harvest to the Sons and Daughters of God

Dr Nteri Nelson   *Nteri Renenet Elson*

Neteru revealing Harvest to the Sons and Daughters of God

This work is a synopsis, derivative, expansion and clarifying of an earlier and more comprehensive work of a similar Title, *Ka Ab Ba Buiding The Lighted Temple.*

The press of Spirit causes this work to go forward now even though it is still undergoing editing phases.

ISBN: 978-0-9659600-1-4

Printed in the United States of America

Published by: The Academy of Kemetic Education & Wellness, Inc. Right Relationship Right Knowledge

53 Cedar St. Mattapan, MA 02126

Editor's Review: Adisa Makalani, Editor, Classic Transcripts

Once more Dr. Nteri Nelson has endeavored to expand the wisdom from the Nile Valley. Delving into beneficent legacy that our ancestors bequeathed us, she probes the Afrikan astronomical, biological, socio-psychological foundation for living.

As with many things in life what seems simple is profound: opposites, dualities and roles of compliment. On closer observation we find that there are not enough lifetimes to comprehend the intricacy of ancestors' wisdom.

Here's hoping you enjoy your journey with Dr. Nteri and know that the joy is in the journey.

This book is dedicated to – AMEN AMENET

Infinite, eternal All in All, Neter, Neteru, Fount of

All Possibility, Spirit that reveals to me.

Dr Nteri Nelson   **Nteri Renenet Elson**
Neteru revealing Harvest to the Sons and Daughters of God

The author is available for group lectures and individual consultations. For further information or to order additional copies contact:

АЖЕ

AЖademy of Kemetic Education & Wellness, INC.

Right Relationship and Right Knowledge

Afrikan Origin of The Ancient/Egyptian Wisdom

Awakening Жonsciousness

Afrikan Жnowledge

Wsir/Ausarian Enlightenment

The Knowledge & Education That Awakens

1st Eye Awareness into

The Metaphysics, Art & Science of Daily Living

Leading to

Spiritual Transformation, Right Relationship,

Soul Purpose Living, & Service
Classes Held at:

53 Cedar St.   Mattapan MA 02126
www.rrrk.net   **(617) 296 -7797**

About the Author:

Terri Nelson, PhD.E, LICSW, MSW, MSEP, Shækem RA АЖЕ (Reiki) Master

aka Nteri Renenet Elson

The Neteru revealing Harvest to the Sons and Daughters of God

Dr. Nteri is a Metaphysician, Teacher of the Afrikan origins of the Ancient wisdom and a Holistic Psychotherapist. She is adjunct Professor in Afrikana studies at the University of Massachusetts in Boston. She is co-founder of, *The Academy of Kemetic Education & Wellness, Right Relationship Right Knowledge, Inc.* where she teaches an Afrikan Centered Model for Psychological, Spiritual and Character development, which is underpinned by the History of Ancient Afrika/Kemet (Egypt) and the Diaspora as a way of Self knowledge, healing and health.

As a licensed clinician, she has worked in the behavioral/mental health field for the last 30 years providing counseling and consultation to individuals, couples, families, groups and agencies. She is an independent researcher, a gifted Symbologist and is a student and teacher of the language, Metu Neter (later called Hieroglyphics by the Greeks).

Her analysis and synthesis within psychological, historical, social, behavioral and metaphysical fields gives deep and penetrative insight into the journey of unfolding consciousness within the human family.

Dr Nteri is author of: *Ka Ab Ba Building The Lighted Temple; Secrets of Race and Consciousness; Afrikan Cosmology Kemet: The Golden Sun Egg Uncracked; Ausar, The Pope, Santa Claus, Christmas, and Christianity; On The Way To Finding Your Soulmate; The Right Relationship Workbook and The Forgiveness Process Workbook.*

She has lectured at numerous conferences nationally and internationally which include: the Association for the Study of Classical Afrikan Civilization (ASCAC); Indigenous Afrikan Healers; First World Alliance; Institute for the Study of Race and Culture; The Nile Valley; Melanin; Sankofa; and Metu Neter Conferences. She is the Massachusetts Region Representative for ASCAC.

KaAbBa: The Great Pyramid is The Tree of Life: MerKaBa

Secrets Revealed in The MerAkhutu

Table of Contents:

Chapter 1 Preview

Chapter 1

Chapter 2

KaAbBa: The Great Pyramid is The Tree of Life: MerKaBa

Secrets Revealed in The MerAkhutu

Appendix

Bibliography

Chapter 1 Preview

This Capstone book, *KaAbBa: The Great Pyramid is The Tree of Life: MerKaBa,* Secrets Revealed in The MerAkhutu, is an eye opener for those with no knowledge of the Tree of Life and a giant leap forward for those who have been seeking advanced knowledge of the Tree of Life. All levels of readers are strongly encouraged in their thorough reading of this book, while gaining knowledge of my earlier larger volume book, *Ka Ab Ba Building The Lighted Temple/The Metaphysical Keys to the Tree of Life,* in which much information has been given about the symbol found on its front cover and pictured on the following page:

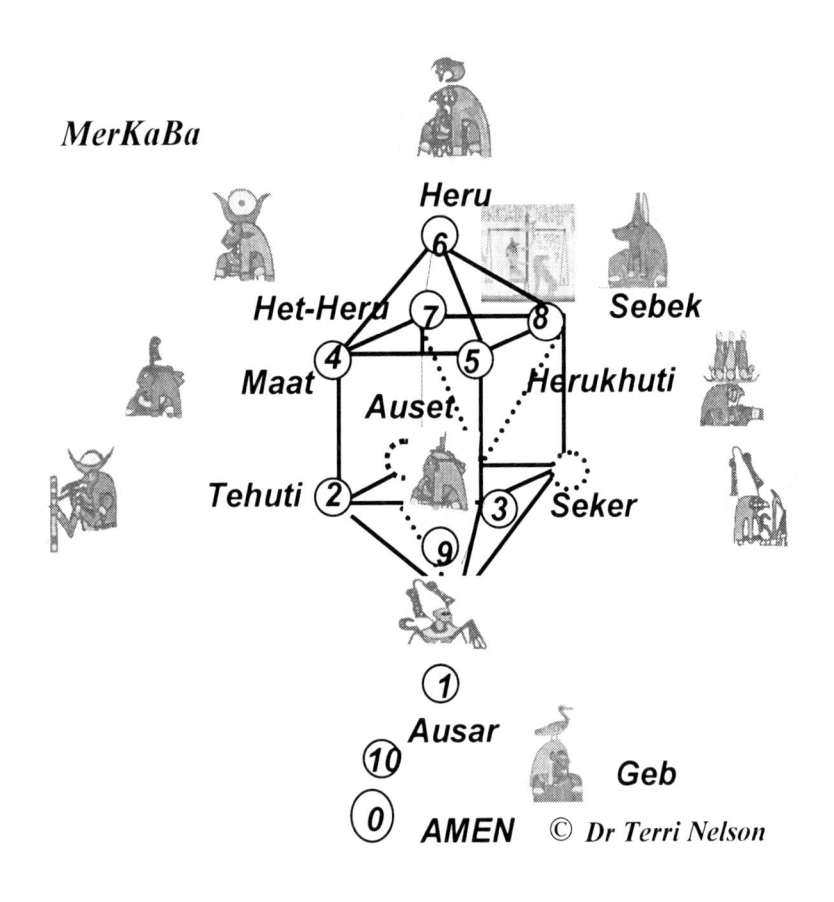

MerKaBa

Heru
6

Het-Heru 7 8 Sebek
4 5
Maat Herukhuti
Auset

Tehuti 2 3 Seker
9

1

Ausar
10
Geb
0 AMEN © Dr Terri Nelson

Cross referencing with this larger volume work as you read along is suggested. Although this symbol had been revealed to me, which I was dutiful to write about in my earlier work, much remained unrevealed, until now. The further unfoldment of this symbol is the purpose of this Capstone book.

Other readings on the Tree of Life, such as, *Metu Neter Vol. 1* by Ra Un Nefer Amen, will assist the reader in understanding information put forth in this Capstone book. This current work, while making reference to my larger volume, is intended to expand on the wisdom that has been given to me through the ancient Pyramid Texts of Kemet and by Spirit, which guides me.

For a review of the meaning and concise definition of the Metu Neter terms, *Ka Ab Ba:*

Continue reading this Preview Chapter 1 and/or refer to the aforementioned, larger volume book, for a fuller explanation

or

Proceed to **Chapter 1**

If you are not in need of this review and are ready to build upon your knowledge of the Tree of Life - *then the subject at hand is immediately entered into by proceeding to Chapter 1 on page 20.*

Metaphysical Key in Consciousness:

▲ **Afrikan Cosmology**

▲ **The Psychological and Spiritual Journey of Unfolding Consciousness**

▲ **Awakening Consciousness Education**

The Kemetians (later called the Egyptians by the Greeks) used picture images or ideagraphs from nature all around them to communicate ideas, which is the language called MTU NTR, MTW NTR, MEDU or METU NETER. These symbols were later called Hieroglyphics by the Greeks. The Metu Neter, *Ka Ab Ba*, are pictured below:

Ka   **Ab**   **Ba**

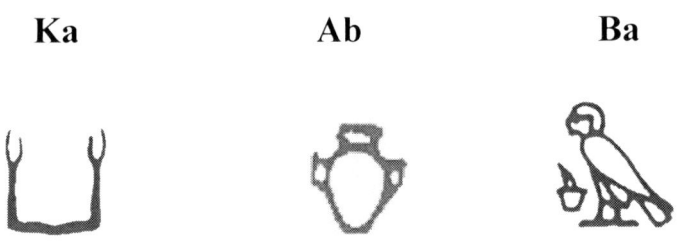

Our Afrikan Ancestors were Masters in the 'Science of the Soul' and 'Journey of the Soul'. They were Master Psychologists and Spiritual Practitioners. They have giving us these 3 primary Metu Neter for:

1. Understanding the Spiritual and Physical Anatomy of Man, Woman and Cosmos
2. Unlocking the Psychological and Spiritual Journey in Unfolding Consciousness

3. Unfettering the Soul from that which would threaten to impede it in its Journey

Why did our Afrikan Ancestors focus within these

3 Primary Metu Neter - *Ka Ab Ba*?

To answer this question the following analogy may best serve. When we 'click onto' an icon on our Windows computer screen, whole documents are opened up and a panorama of information is revealed to our poised and awaiting mind or mental field. By analogy, the 3 primary Metu Neter are like these icons which were used by our Kemetic Ancestors. As we 'click' in turn onto the Metu Neter *Ka, Ab*, and *Ba*, the Psychological and Spiritual Journey in Unfolding Consciousness is revealed. These ideagraphs or pictures are the 'divine idea and speech' which open our 1st eye and aid us to glimpse the Whole Moving Geometry within in the Mind of God/NeterNeteru. Thus, as the Journey unfolds, we are able to see the changing states in our consciousness which lead to changing states in our physical World.

On the Psycho/Spiritual Journey in Unfolding Consciousness what are you as the Sun-Son/Daughter becoming fully conscious of?

For the Kemetians Ka means Spirit. In the Metaphysical Keys that follow, you will see that, Ka – Spirit, takes of the substance of ITSELF to see ITSELF in form. Ka – Spirit, takes of the substance of ITSELF to have consciousness in form. Ka – Spirit, takes of the substance of ITSELF and begins to differentiate itself in/as Spirit-matter. This is one of the many divine paradoxes. As much as Spirit is UNLIMITED and UNCONDITIONED it asserts its right to limit itself in form or matter in order to gain conscious experience of ITSELF. In various grades of material form, IT – Ka, sees ITSELF. It is in *the seeing of ITSELF* that consciousness is born. Thus we are made divine and human, Spiritual and material. For the Kemetians, Ba means Soul and Soul is consciousness. We are told that Ka - Spirit precedes Ba Soul. This is expressed in the following accordingly: Alvin Boyd Kuhn, *The Lost Light*, p. 588.

"The Ba comes forth upon earth to do the will of its Ka.

This is derived from the Ritual Text of the *Prt Em Hru* which is expressed accordingly: E.A. Wallis Budge. *The Egyptian Book of the Dead*, p. 359.

The souls come forth to do the will of their Ka's and the soul of Ausar Ani cometh forth to do the will of his Ka.

The Soul-Ba comes forth upon the Earth to do the will of its Spirit-Ka. For the Kemetians Ab symbolizes the human heart. The heart is the seat of the Soul. It is the conscience and growing consciousness. In this growing

SELF conscious identity, the Ab Soul is the conscious experience of how Spirit and Matter are relating. As man's consciousness develops he must also develop a 'conscience'. This is Heru or the Karest/Christ principle within you that guides you to be and act in accord with the Universal Law of Right Relationship. Through the relating aspect of Ab, the 'seeming' duality between Spirit-Matter with its myriad objective forms in play and display as Ba Ka are seen as ONE. *Ka*Ba is Unconscious-Consciousness and cannot be separated. All 'seeming' divisions between Ka and Ba are arbitrary and merely useful for helping us to find our way back *Home* from a Spiritual Journey in Unfolding Consciousness that we never really went on, except in an illusion we came to believe as 'Real.' Thus through Ab Soul consciousness the same One True Self is seen in every other Self. This is expressed in the diagram at below: Further detail is given throughout this Capstone book and in the larger volume work, *Ka Ab Ba Building The Lighted Temple.*

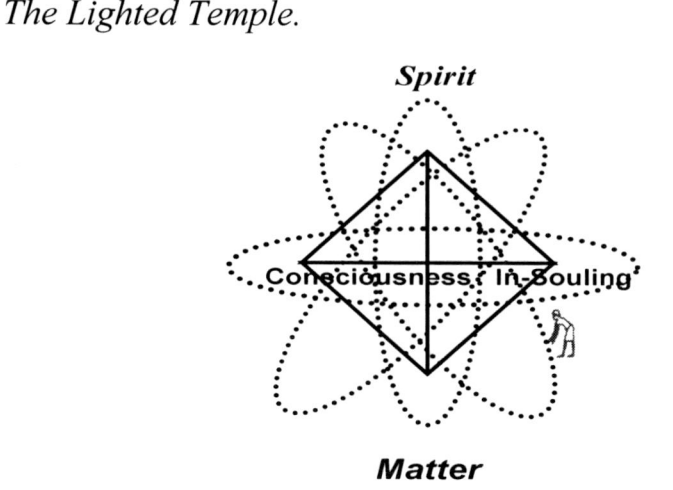

Spirit

Con¢ciousness, In-Souling'

Matter

KaAbBa: The Great Pyramid is The Tree of Life: MerKaBa

Secrets Revealed in The MerAkhutu

As Heru, we are Sun-Son/Daughter. On our Psycho/Spiritual Journey in Unfolding Consciousness as Heru - sphere 6 in the Tree of Life, we make our descent into material life conditions. On our return journey, we make our hard, arduous climb of re-ascent Home again, into the Spiritual realms. You are becoming fully conscious of the perfect relationship between Father and Mother and Spirit and Matter. To become fully conscious is to live the consciousness of Ausar Ba and Auset Ka - that we are made in the Image and Likeness of God and All SELVES are but the ONE True Indivisible SELF.

By following and reclaiming their ways the Ancestors have taught me to be a Kemetic Psychologist and Spiritual Practitioner. As we make a shift in consciousness now in this World period as indicated in chapter 17, Understanding What Time It Is, *Ka Ab Ba Building The Lighted Temple/The Metaphysical Keys to the Tree of Life,* let us peer within the wisdom of our Afrikan Ancestors for utmost guidance in navigating our way.

Chapter 1

▲ MerAkhutu The Great Pyramid of Khufu

The Great Pyramid of Giza, is called the MerAkhutu, in the Kemetic language of Metu Neter. It was built by the Nesut Bity (King), Khufu.

The purpose of this book is to reveal that:

1) The Great Pyramid of Giza is a symbol of the Tree of Life.

2) The Great Pyramid of Giza is a symbol of the MerKaBa.

The further unfoldment of these symbols, the Great Pyramid, the Tree of Life, and the MerKaBa are given through the Metaphysical Keys that follow and are introduced in each instance as such, by the following header:

Metaphysical Key in Consciousness:

Let us now first examine the Tree of Life.

When I first wrote the book, *Ka Ab Ba Building The Lighted Temple*, I was writing about the Tree of Life. Spirit revealed to me at the time that:

Metaphysical Key in Consciousness:

▲The Tree of Life is *likewise*, a symbol of the MerKaBa and Great Pyramid. How does the Tree of Life become this symbol?

To deal with this matter structurally and geometrically, the Tree of Life 'bends back' circularly upon itself, like the yogic Nut pose, the serpent swallowing its tail or the Kemetic dancer/acrobat. In the bending of the Tree of Life circularly, we see the MerKaBa and Great Pyramid forming. This is pictured, on the two next pages:

Neteru revealing Harvest to the Sons and Daughters of God

▲The Tree of Life

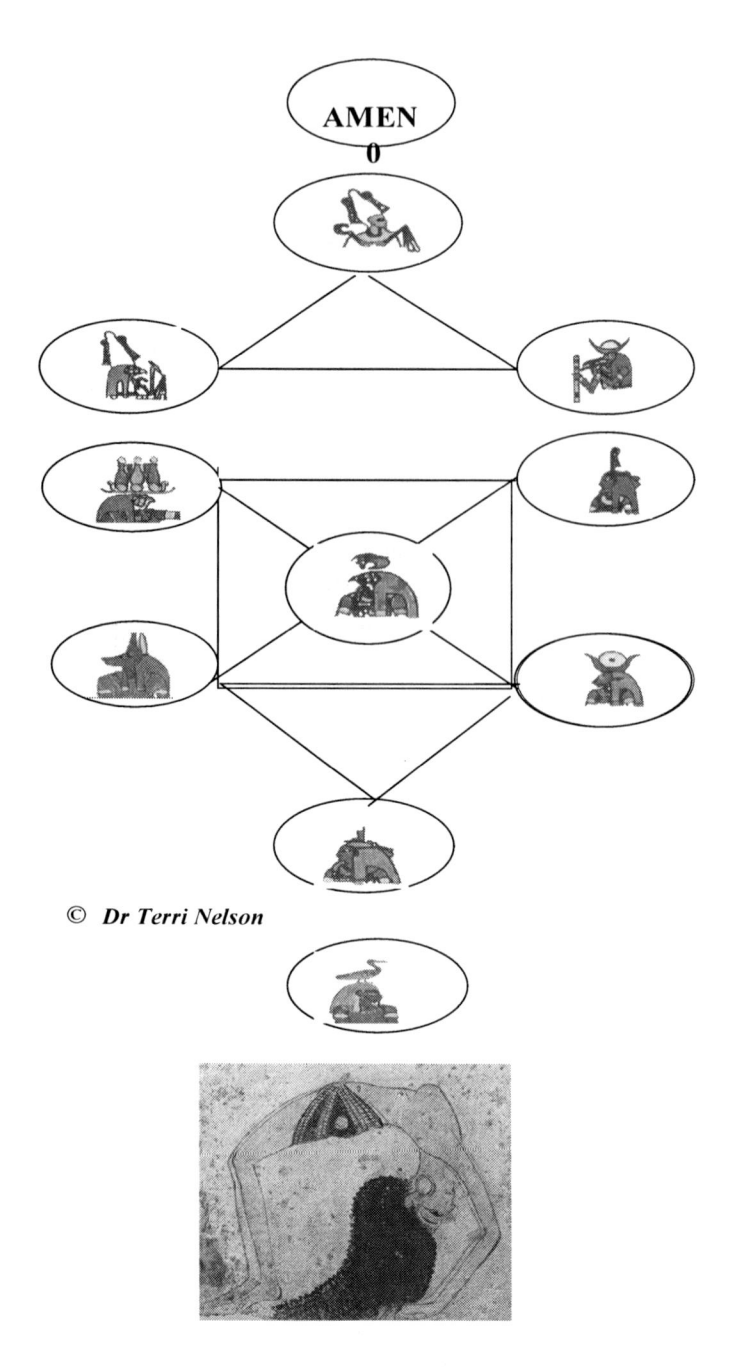

© *Dr Terri Nelson*

KaAbBa: The Great Pyramid is The Tree of Life: MerKaBa
Secrets Revealed in The MerAkhutu

▲ The MerKaBa
▲ KaAbBa

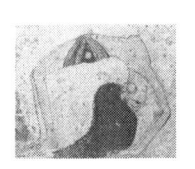

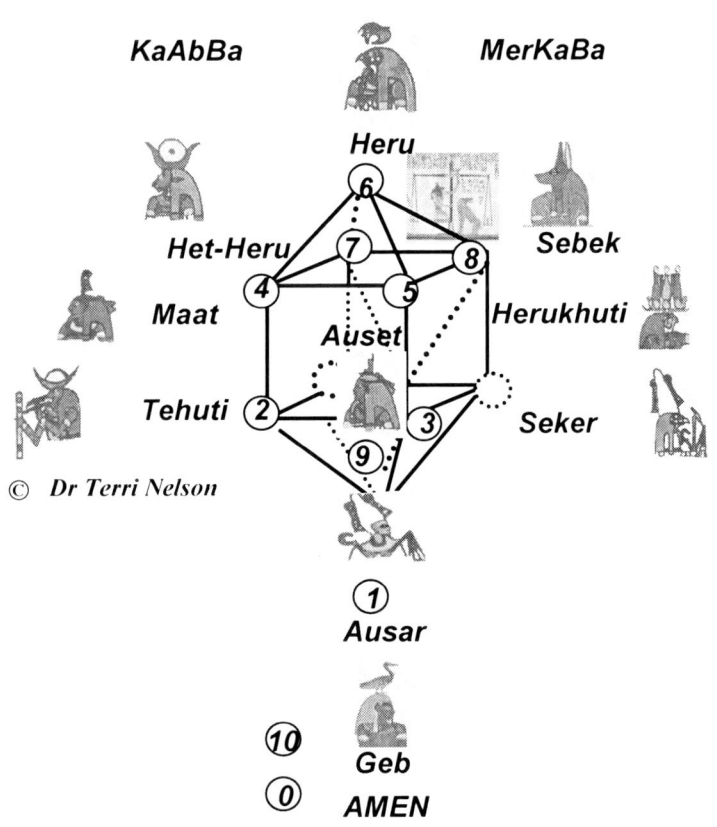

Tree of Life Great Pyramid MerAkhutu

KaAbBa   MerKaBa

Heru

Het-Heru   Sebek

Maat   Herukhuti

Auset

Tehuti   Seker

© Dr Terri Nelson

① Ausar

⑩
Geb
⓪ AMEN

Paut Neteru, Solar Bark, Chariot of the Gods

23

As mentioned, Spirit had revealed this MerKaBa symbol to me when I wrote the book, *KaAbBa Building The Lighted Temple/The Metaphysical Keys to the Tree of Life.* It was placed on the front cover and I was dutiful to write much about it, although much remained unrevealed, until now. At that time, I would then go on in my book to describe the Tree of Life both, 'linearly' or laid out in a straight line fashion and 'circularly and spherically'

Metaphysical Key in Consciousness:

▲ The Tree of Life

▲ The Ka Ab Ba

The reader would at first, learn about the basic configuration of the Tree of Life into its three primary triangles, Ka Ab Ba pictured as follows:

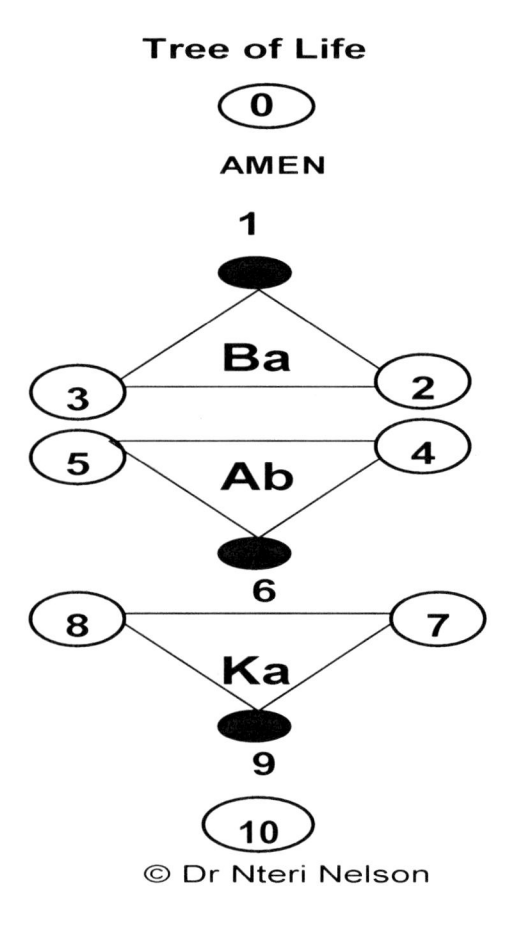

© Dr Nteri Nelson

Metaphysical Key in Consciousness:

▲ The Divine Trinity of Ausar Auset Heru

▲ The Ka Ab Ba

The Divine Trinity of Ausar Auset and Heru and their correspondence with Ka Ab Ba are described in great detail throughout the book, *KaAbBa Building The Lighted Temple:The Metaphysical Keys to the Tree of Life*. Here we see the Divine Trinity of Kemet that existed long before Christianity. Ausar is in the center, with wife Auset at right and son Heru at left pictured below:

Ka Ab Ba corresponds with the Divine Trinity of Auset, Heru and Ausar respectively and are revealed here in the 'linear' Tree of Life, in the diagram below:

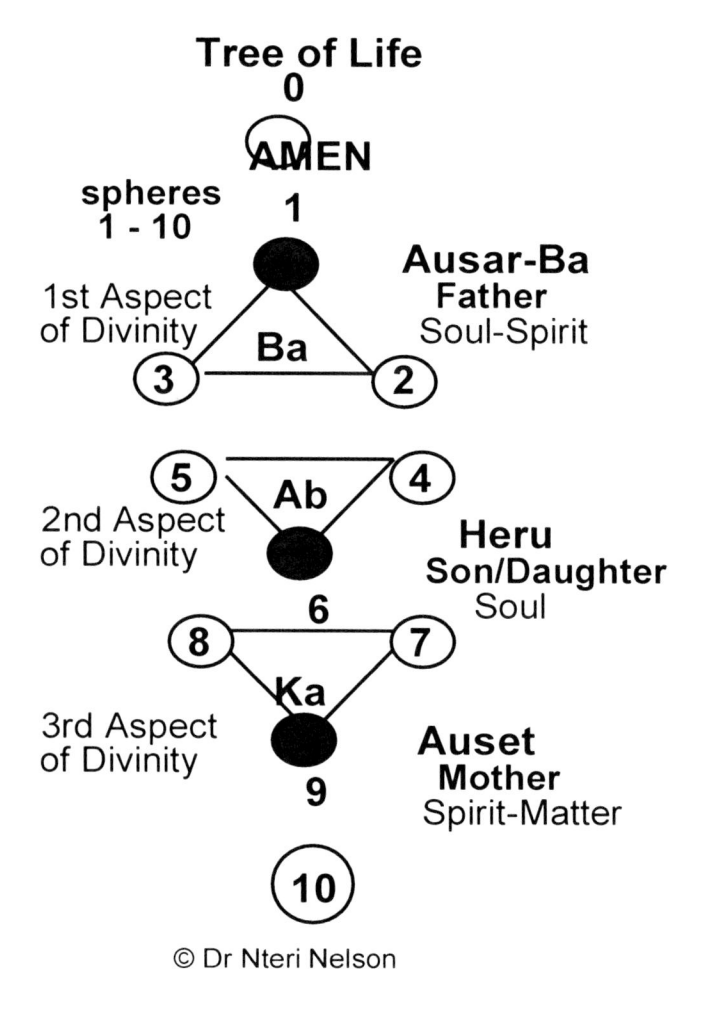

© Dr Nteri Nelson

Neteru revealing Harvest to the Sons and Daughters of God

By the end of the book, *KaAbBa Building The Lighted Temple:The Metaphysical Keys to the Tree of Life,* the three primary triangles, Ka Ab Ba, the square of the Ka-erect–or/Personality, the Paut Neteru spheres 0 – 10, and many systems of divine and human unfoldment had been revealed within the Tree of Life to the reader, indicated in the 'Big Map' (10), and shown on the next page as follows:

Metaphysical Key in Consciousness:

▲ The Tree of Life 'Big Map'

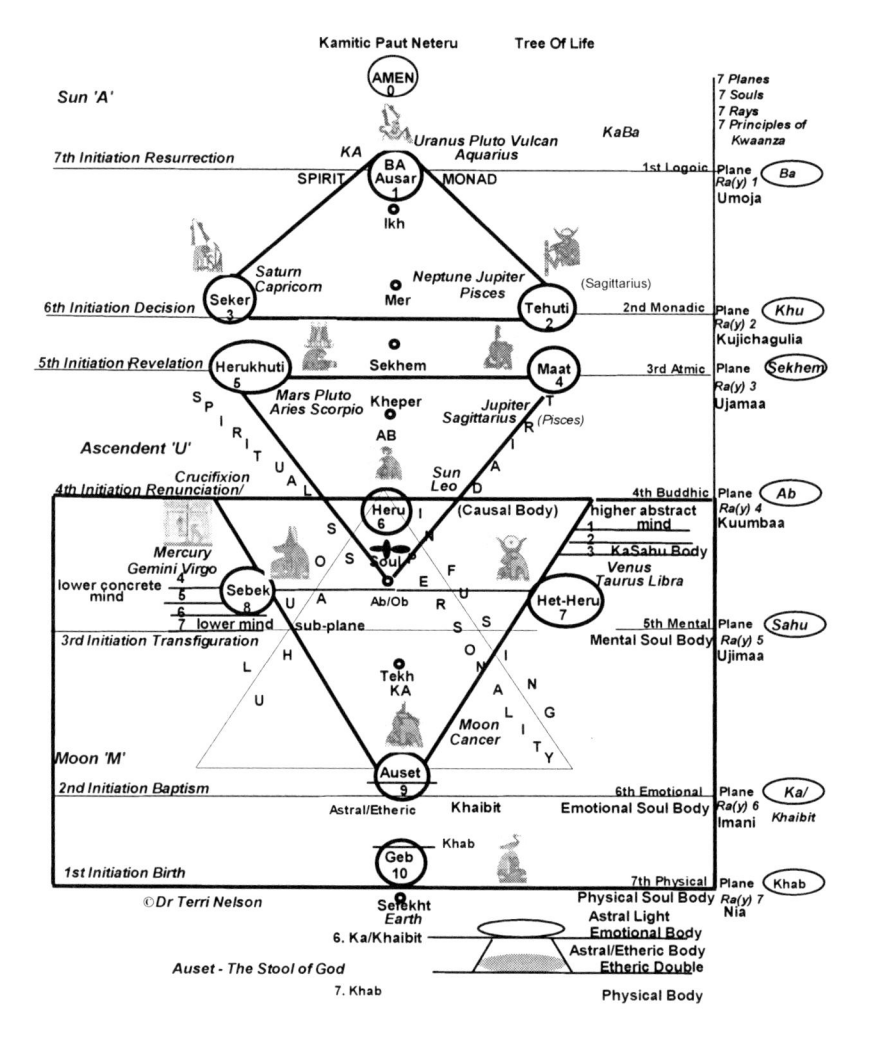

©Dr Terri Nelson

29

> Metaphysical Key in Consciousness:

▲ The Tree of Life and the Tamarisk Tree

Where does the symbol of the Tree derive from? One source is seen in the following as Auset travels to Byblos in search of her deceased husband Ausar, which is expressed accordingly: E. A. Budge, *The Prt Em Hru (Egyptian Book Of The Dead)*, p.l.

> Soon after she learned that the chest [read here: sarcophagus] had been carried by the sea to Byblos, where it had been gently laid by the waves among the branches of a **Tamarisk** tree, which in a very short time had grown to a magnificent size and had enclosed the chest within its trunk. The king of the country, admiring the tree, cut it down and made a **pillar** for the roof of his house of that part which contained the body of Ausar.

In a different account the story is continued accordingly: E. A. Budge, *Osiris. The Egyptian Religion and Resurrection*, p. 5.

> Meanwhile the waves had carried the box to the coast of Syria and cast it up at Byblos, and soon as it rested on the ground a large

Erica tree sprang up, and growing all round the box enclosed it on every side. The king of Byblos marveled at the size of this **tree,** and had it cut down, and caused a **pillar** for his palace to be made of that portion of the trunk which contained the **box.**

When this news reached Auset she set out at once for Byblos, and when she arrived there she sat down by the side of the fountain of the palace and spoke to no one except the queen's maidens, who soon came to her. These she treated with great courtesy, and talked graciously to them, and caressed them, and tired their head, and at the same time transferred to them wonderful **odour** of her own body. When the maidens returned to the palace the queen perceived the **odour** which emanated from their hair and bodies, and learning from them that it was due to their contact with Auset, she sent to her and invited her to come to the palace.

After a conversation with her she appointed her to be the nurse of one of her children. Auset gave the child her finger instead of her breast to suck, and at night she burned away in fire his mortal parts, whilst she herself, in the form of a swallow flew around and around the pillar which contained the body of Ausar, uttering mournful chirpings. After she had treated the child thus for some time, the queen one night saw her son burning in the fire, whereupon she uttered a piercing cry, and so prevented him from obtaining the gift of immortality which was about to be bestowed upon him.

Let's dispell the word tamarisk:

Derived Word List:

Kristmas, C(h)ristmas – as in Christmas Tree.

Meaning:

The word Tamarisk reveals the word Christmas. It is the Tree symbolizing how you 'erect-Ka'. The story also reveals the word Eureka which is to express triumph upon finding or discovering something. The greatest find we can make is to discover the SELF. In both instances, the Evergreen Tree symbolizes eternal life. It is the Ka-rest-mas Tree that is later called the Christmas Tree. So we may see from our story that:

1. Immortality comes from successively raising the fires of Ra up the spinal column. The djed/Tet pillar and the spinal column are likewise symbols of the Tree of Life.

2. This is our elevator ride up the djed/Tet Pillar through the 7 planes of consciousness (these are further illustrated on pages 118-120).
3. By moving through the fires we purify our mortal parts. The Tree of Life is pictured below:

The Tamarisk Tree of Kemet, Afrika

© Vladimir Melnik shutterstock.com

The Erica Tree of Life infolding the body of Ausar.

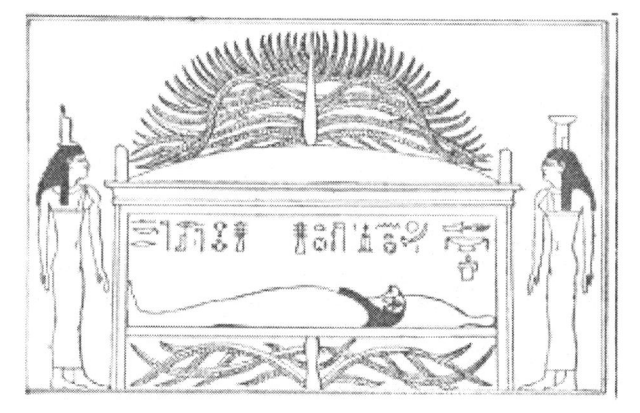

© Ausar The Egyptian Religion of Resurrection

Let us now examine the MerKaBa. When I speak about MerKaBa, I am not making any reference here to what is also called MerKaBa and looks like this:

I find little, if any resonance with this symbol and this book makes no reference to it at all. This symbol suggests a modified, incomplete derivative effort, similar to the 10 Commandments, which takes some of the Kemetic laws of Ma'at, and leaves the rest. Instead we bring our awareness to this MerKaBa symbol which is the Great Pyramid (MerAkhutu) of Khufu, Nesut Bity (King) of Kemet, pictured as follows:

Metaphysical Key in Consciousness:

▲ The Great Pyramid is the MerKaBa

▲The Sacred Geometry, linear, circular, spherical, triangular, etc.

Revealed is:

The MerKaBa, which is the Great Pyramid of Kemet, brings in all the geometrical arrangement - linear, circular, square, spherical, triangular, etc. As mentioned, Spirit had revealed to me then, that the Tree of Life 'bends back' circularly upon itself and in this bending the Great Pyramid and the MerKaBa are revealed. Here we see the double pyramid, one above and one below, with a perfect square in between (the quaternary) where character (Ka-Ra-acter/Ka-erect-er) is fashioned and is likewise the *tomb* and the *womb* of rebirth. The MerKaBa when rounded, be-comes a sphere. This is pictured on the two following pages:

Neteru revealing Harvest to the Sons and Daughters of God

Tree of Life Great Pyramid MerAkhutu

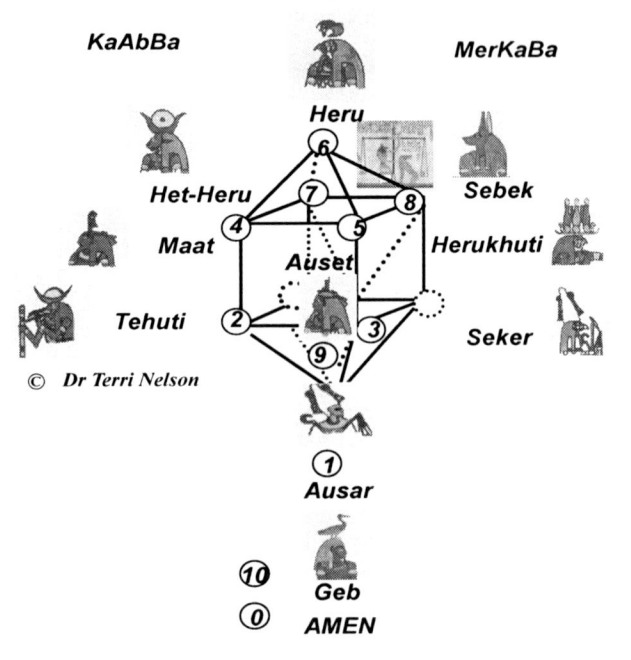

KaAbBa: The Great Pyramid is The Tree of Life: MerKaBa

Secrets Revealed in The MerAkhutu

For sometime, I have been meditating within:

▲The MerKaBa, *that is* the Tree of Life, that is the Great Pyramid MerAkhutu

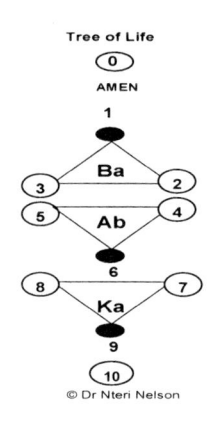

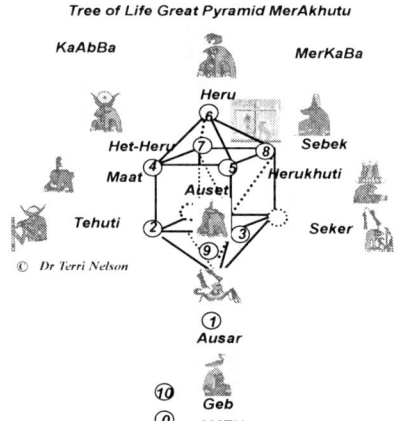

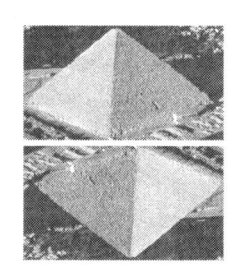

Chapter 2

Metaphysical Key in Consciousness:

Revealed is:

▲ The Paut Neteru/The Chariot of the Gods

The MerKaBa is the Paut Neteru, the Chariot of the Gods. It is our Spiritual equipment or faculty, which is both human and divine. We are and have access to the Paut Neteru, the company of the Gods, and all of their divine qualities.

KaAbBa: The Great Pyramid is The Tree of Life: MerKaBa
Secrets Revealed in The MerAkhutu

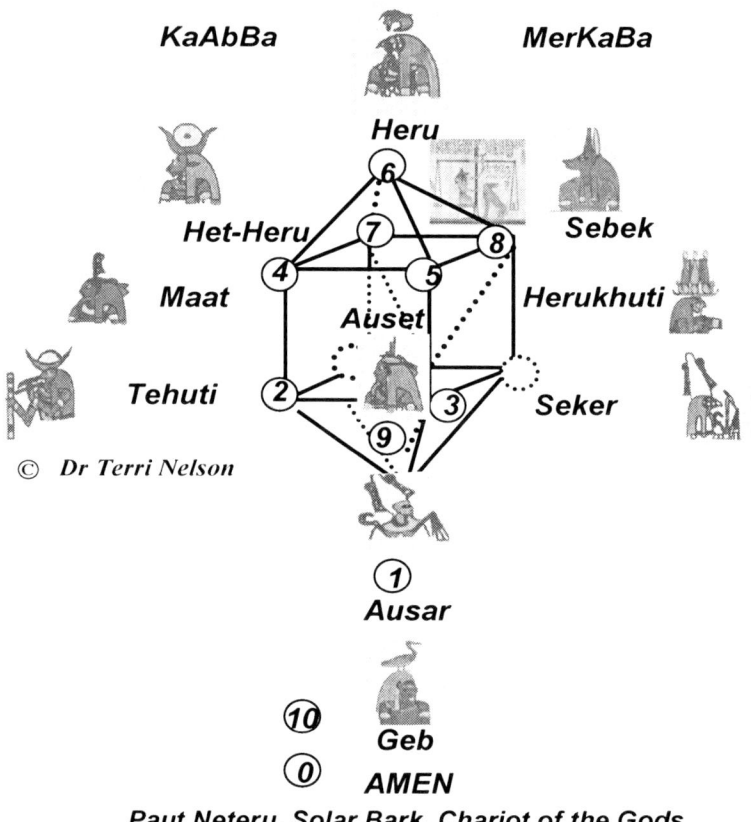

Tree of Life Great Pyramid MerAkhutu

KaAbBa   Heru   MerKaBa

Het-Heru   Sebek

Maat   Herukhuti

Auset

Tehuti   Seker

© Dr Terri Nelson

Ausar

Geb

AMEN

Paut Neteru, Solar Bark, Chariot of the Gods

Metaphysical Key in Consciousness:

▲ The Resurrection of the Sun - Son/Daughter

The Karest

Revealed is:

In the bending back of the Tree of Life, we see, Sphere 6, Heru, Ab triangle, Sun, Sign of Leo, the heart - coming to the apex of the Great Pyramid the Mer Akhutu, as indicated by the arrow. This rising *is* the Resurrection of the Sun – Son/Daughter - The Karest. This is seen in the diagram on the following page:

KaAbBa: The Great Pyramid is The Tree of Life: MerKaBa
Secrets Revealed in The MerAkhutu

Tree of Life Great Pyramid MerAkhutu

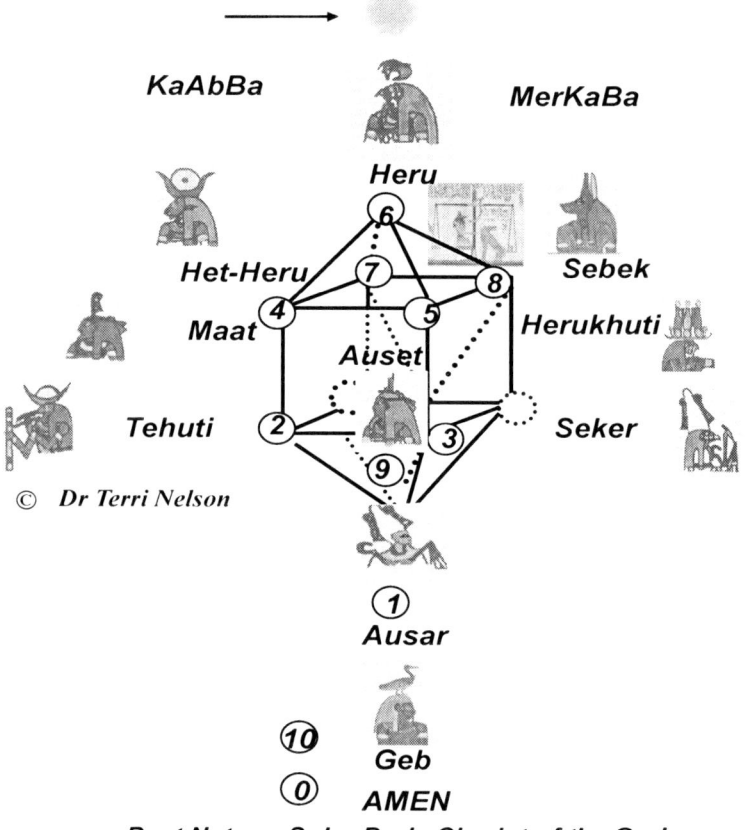

KaAbBa

MerKaBa

Heru

Het-Heru

Sebek

Maat

Herukhuti

Auset

Tehuti

Seker

© Dr Terri Nelson

Ausar

Geb

AMEN

Paut Neteru, Solar Bark, Chariot of the Gods

41

Metaphysical Key in Consciousness:

▲The Lighted Temple, The Solar Bark

Revealed is:

The Book, *KaAbBa Building The Lighted Temple*, is a book dedicated toward the purpose of just that, Building the Lighted Temple. When we as Son/Daughter are able to come over the horizon like the Sun and reach the zenith, then the temple we have built is Light-filled. It is the Solar Bark, and we have become solarized or luminous beings in a luminous 'body' of Light.

Metaphysical Key in Consciousness:

▲The Mesu Heru 4 Sons of Heru

We also see the 4 Mesu Heru (sons of Heru) represented as spheres 4 Ma'at, 5 Herukhuti, 7 Het-Heru and 8 Sebek.

Metaphysical Key in Consciousness:

▲The Union and Divine Marriage of Ausar Ba and Auset Ka

In a straight line, immediately below sphere 6 Heru Ab Sun/Son-Daughter, we see sphere 9 Auset Ka Divine Mother and sphere 1 Ausar Ba Divine Father, coming together circularly, in embrace. This is indicated by the arrows in the following diagram:

KaAbBa: The Great Pyramid is The Tree of Life: MerKaBa
Secrets Revealed in The MerAkhutu

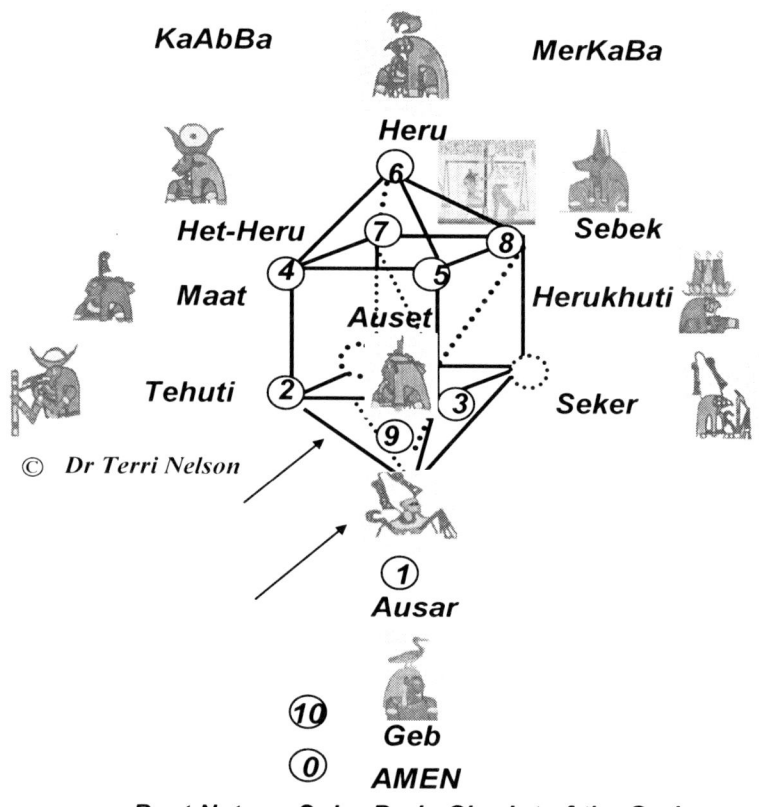

Tree of Life Great Pyramid MerAkhutu

KaAbBa

MerKaBa

Heru

Het-Heru

Maat

Auset

Tehuti

Sebek

Herukhuti

Seker

© Dr Terri Nelson

Ausar

Geb

AMEN

Paut Neteru, Solar Bark, Chariot of the Gods

Specifically, we turn our attention to the next diagram of the Great Pyramid which reveals the hidden chambers of the King and Queen as follows:

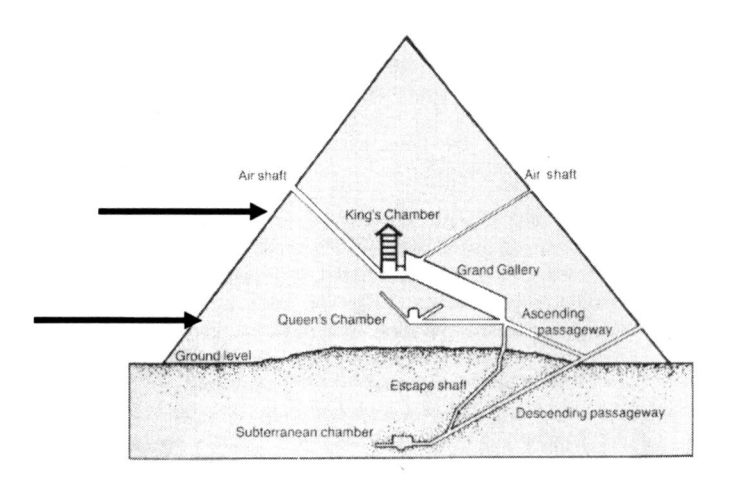

Metaphysical Key in Consciousness:

▲The King and Queen Chambers of The Great Pyramid of Khufu symbolize

▲Ka Auset, Ba Ausar, the Divine Marriage of Auset Ausar

Revealed is:

Notice that in the MerKaBa, Ausar and Auset, the King and Queen are also brought together in secret embrace in the chamber(s) below:

KaAbBa: The Great Pyramid is The Tree of Life: MerKaBa

Secrets Revealed in The MerAkhutu

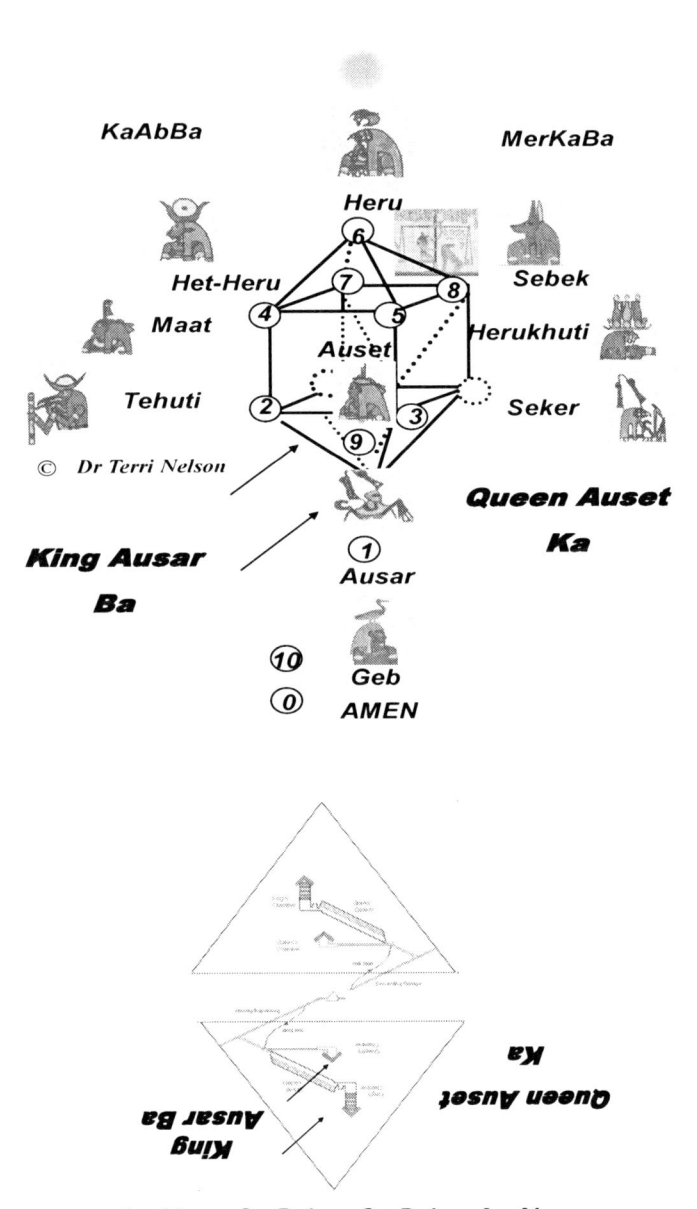

As Above So Below, So Below As Above

> Metaphysical Key in Consciousness:

▲Kemetic Law: As Above, So Below, So Below, As Above

Here, we are seeing the Kemetic Law As Above, So Below, So Below As Above, reflected. Our Afrikan ancestors of the Nile Valley have left us this symbol of the Great Pyramid, the MerAkhutu, revealing that which is happening on Earth is also reflected in our own Spiritual faculty, our monumental temple building, which is both human and divine. The monument that is with(in) us is the monument with(out), that is the Great Pyramid. We are likewise, building the monument of the Lighted Temple.

▲ KaBa are One

As referenced here from, *Ka Ab Ba Building The Lighted Temple* p, 80:

For the Kemetians Ka means Spirit and Ba means Soul. We are told that Ka precedes Ba. This is expressed in the following accordingly: Alvin Boyd Kuhn, *The Lost Light*, p. 588.

"The Ba comes forth upon earth to do the will of its Ka.

KaAbBa: The Great Pyramid is The Tree of Life: MerKaBa
Secrets Revealed in The MerAkhutu

This is derived from the Ritual Text of the *Prt Em Hru* which is expressed accordingly: E.A. Wallis Budge. *The Egyptian Book of the Dead*, p. 359.

> The souls come forth to do the will of their Ka's and the soul of Ausar Ani cometh forth to do the will of his Ka.

The above quotes may be re-stated as follows:

The Soul-Ba comes forth upon the Earth to do the will of its Spirit-Ka.

*Ka*Ba As Unity. What is the arising of the Number 1?

What we must remember is that *Ka*Ba is Unconscious-Consciousness and cannot be separated. This Unity is expressed in the diagram that follows:

Metaphysical Key in Consciousness:

▲ Unitive Consciousness

As seen, *Ka*Ba enfold and circle upon each other, like the serpent that bites its own tail. Where one ends and the other begins, challenging our ability to discern. All 'seeming' divisions between Ka and Ba are arbitrary and merely useful for helping us to find our way back *Home* from a Spiritual Journey in Unfolding Consciousness that we never really went on, except in an illusion, which we came to believe as 'Real.'

Ka and Ba as a 'seeming' Duality. What is the arising of the Number 2?

According to Albert Churchward, *Signs & Symbols of Primordial Man,* p. 211.

> This [the duality, the first differentiation] was the original, and the Egyptians worked out from this first two things – that is, the Ka, the Spirit, and the Ba, the Soul.

Metaphysical Key in Consciousness:

▲ The Ka Ab Ba

▲ Spirit-Matter Continuum

For the Kemetians Ab symbolizes the human heart. The heart is the seat of the Soul, the conscience and growing Self conscious identity. The Ab Soul is the conscious experience of how Spirit and Matter are relating. As man's consciousness develops he must also develop a 'conscience'. This is Heru or the Karest/Christ principle within you that guides you to be and act in accord with the Universal Law of Right Relationship.

Through the relating aspect of Ab, the 'seeming' duality between Spirit-Matter with its myriad objective forms in play and display as Ba and Ka are seen as ONE. Thus through Ab Soul consciousness, the same One True Self is seen in every other Self.

Trinity

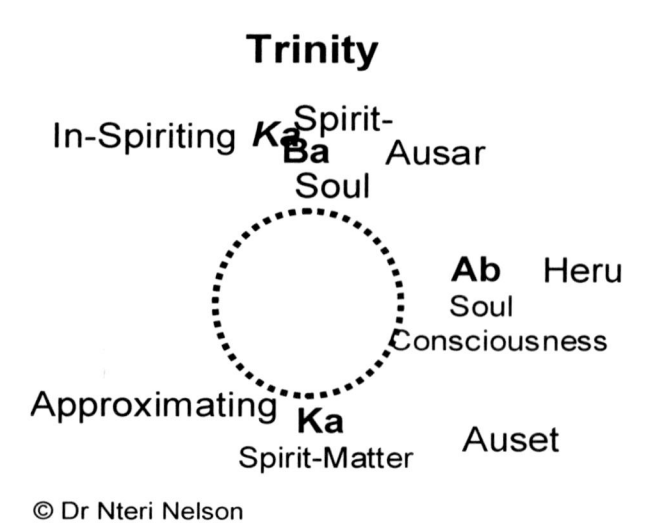

© Dr Nteri Nelson

This is expressed in the diagrams above and on the next page. On our Psycho/Spiritual Journey in Unfolding Consciousness as Heru - sphere 6 in the Tree of Life, we make our descent into material life conditions. As Heru we are Sun-Son/Daughter. On our return journey, we make our hard, arduous climb of re-ascent Home again, into the Spiritual realms.

Spirit

Consciousness: In-Souling

Matter

You are becoming fully conscious of the perfect relationship between Father and Mother, Spirit and Matter. To become fully conscious is to live the consciousness of Ausar Ba Auset Ka - that we are made in the Image and Likeness of Neter Neteru, God and All SELVES are but the ONE True Indivisible SELF.

Metaphysical Key in Consciousness:

▲ MerKaBa

▲ There is no death

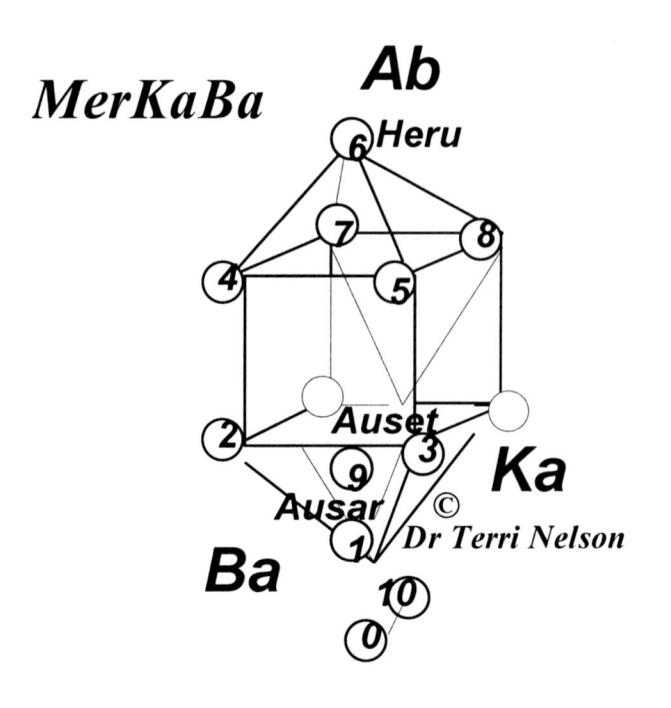

In MerKaBa consciousness there is no death. There is only the transmigration of the Soul from life into greater Life. Death is the seeming discontinuity of conscious-ness – a cutting into pieces of the ALL Consciousness. This is symbolized as the broken body of Ausar, cut into fourteen parts.

At each seeming 'death' the initiate appears again and again within the Hall of Amenta, that his heart may be weighed and thereby tested. Each time his heart has fallen short of being as light as the feather of Ma'at, he has to mount again the wheel of birth and death and fall back into the material realm.

This cycle repeats itself as we undergo the Initiatory process. Higher states of consciousness are achieved – until the state of Unitive, Neteru or God Conscious is the stabilized Realization. The initiate finally stands within the Hall of Amenta and is _found_ *Maa Kheru.* Thus, you are justified as living in truth, morally and in total equilibrium with the laws of God.

Metaphysical Key in Consciousness:

▲ Unitive Consciousness, God Consciousness

▲ The 3 Primary Qualities of Consciousness/ Mind

▲ The Great Egg of Consciousness

What is a state of Unitive, Neteru or God Consciousness? Let us review the book, *KaAbBa Building The Lighted Temple:The Metaphysical Keys to the Tree of Life* p. 154 -160, as follows:

The 3 primary Egg or Egoic States in Consciousness may be observed as follows:

1. Consciousness may remain Unitive
2. Consciousness may become Dualized and Reconciliative/Combative
3. Consciousness may become Particularized or Separative into many parts

How we perceive the 'outer World' depends upon which of these 3 primary Egoic states we find ourselves identified with. The qualities each expresses is shown in the following diagram:

The Great Egg of Consciousness

3 Primary Egoic States of Consciousness

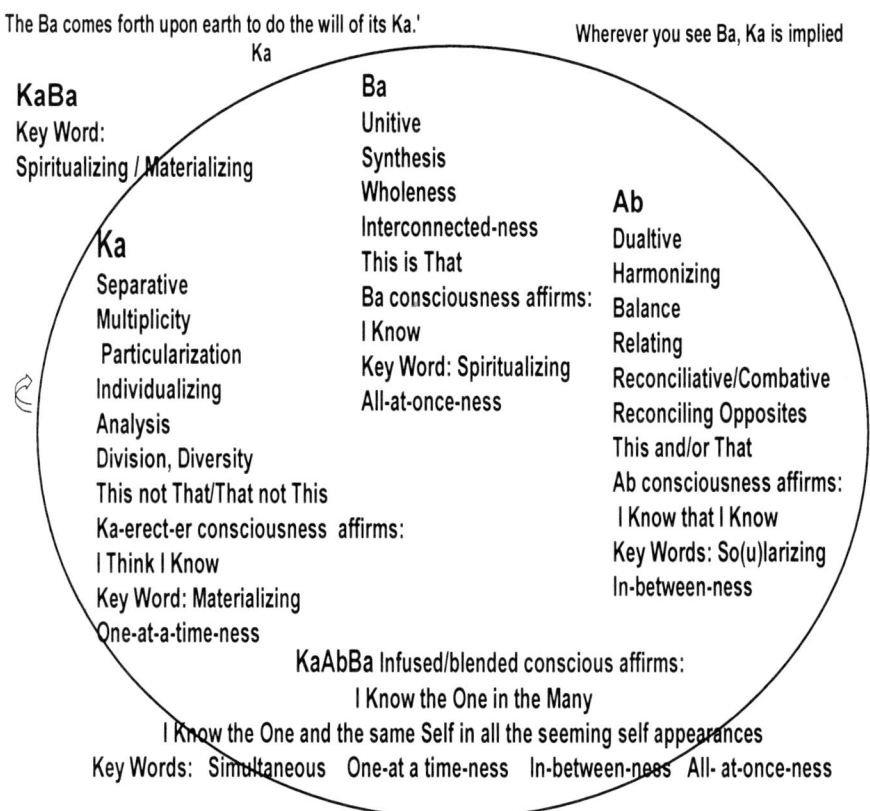

The Ba comes forth upon earth to do the will of its Ka.'
Ka

Wherever you see Ba, Ka is implied

KaBa
Key Word:
Spiritualizing / Materializing

Ba
Unitive
Synthesis
Wholeness
Interconnected-ness
This is That
Ba consciousness affirms:
I Know
Key Word: Spiritualizing
All-at-once-ness

Ka
Separative
Multiplicity
Particularization
Individualizing
Analysis
Division, Diversity
This not That/That not This
Ka-erect-er consciousness affirms:
I Think I Know
Key Word: Materializing
One-at-a-time-ness

Ab
Dualtive
Harmonizing
Balance
Relating
Reconciliative/Combative
Reconciling Opposites
This and/or That
Ab consciousness affirms:
I Know that I Know
Key Words: So(u)larizing
In-between-ness

KaAbBa Infused/blended conscious affirms:
I Know the One in the Many
I Know the One and the same Self in all the seeming self appearances
Key Words: Simultaneous   One-at a time-ness   In-between-ness   All- at-once-ness

© *Dr Terri Nelson*

55

Metaphysical Key in Consciousness:

▲ Pyramidal Power of MerKaBa

When we are within MerKaBa we have access and are using all 3 states of consciousness, seamlessly and effortlessly. We have developed the 1st eye which sees:

> One At A Timeness
>
> In Betweeness and
>
> Simultaneous, All At Once-ness

We possess Spherical Sightedness.

Metaphysical Key in Consciousness:

▲ Geb Earth, Absolving within Amen/Nu(n)

As we move beyond the union and Divine Marriage of AusarBa and AusetKa, in a straight line below, we see - sphere 10 Geb, Earth, the physical body, coming together circularly in embrace and absolving into sphere 0 Amen - from which it arose. This is pictured on the following page:

▲ The Union of Geb and Nu(t)

▲ The Masonic Symbol

This is also the union of Geb and Nu(t) coming together in embrace, as Geb Earth and Nut Heaven/Sky are One. Geb, the Neter of Earth is pictured at left, lying underneath his wife Nut, Goddess of the sky. Shu (not shown) is the God of air between the couple. Notice the correspondence with the Masonic symbol pictured at right, below:

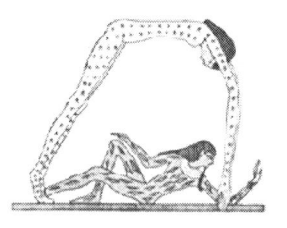 

This is occurring as Heru Ab, the Son-Daughter is becoming as the Sun. Ab, which is also the heart, becomes as radiant as the Sun (the word Earth dispelled is the word 'heart' (see *Ka Ab Ba Building The Lighted Temple*). Heaven and Earth are brought together as the human heart has been solarized, As Above, So Below, So Below as Above. As Heru, you are the Sun – Son/Daughter who comes to dwell on Earth. This is pictured on the following page:

Tree of Life Great Pyramid MerAkhutu

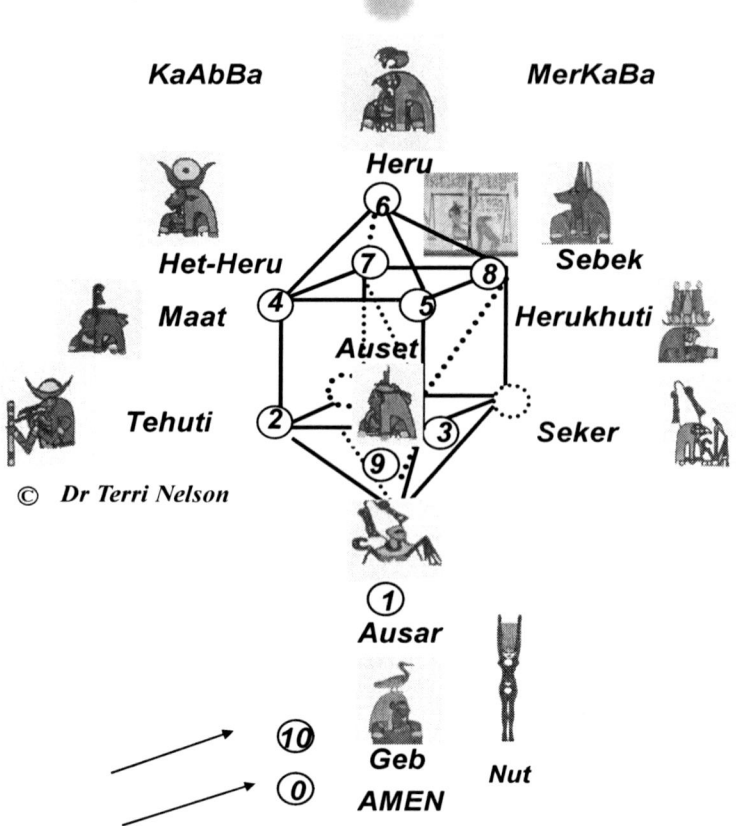

KaAbBa   **MerKaBa**

Heru

Het-Heru   **Sebek**

Maat

Auset

Tehuti   **Seker**

© *Dr Terri Nelson*

Ausar

Geb   **Nut**

AMEN

Paut Neteru, Solar Bark, Chariot of the Gods

Metaphysical Key in Consciousness:

▲Kemet Cosmology, Geb and Nut produce the Great Egg

In Kemet Cosmology, Geb and Nut produced the Great Egg from which the Sun-god sprang. Again pictured at right, we see the Golden Goose on the head of Geb. The Goose/Gander - like Khepera, like the Black Man/Woman, like the Neg (Bull/Cow) - is a symbol of fertility, virility and generativity.

The goose eggs, symbolize the birth of humanity, or more accurately, the individual and collective consciousness of humanity. Geb is one of the company of the Neteru who watch the weighing of the heart of the deceased in the Judgment Hall of Ausar. He provides the righteous with the necessary words of power to enable them to make their escape from the Earth wherein their bodies were laid, but the wicked were held fast by Geb (Seb, Keb). Geb would hold imprisoned the Souls of the wicked, that they might not ascend to Heaven (see *Secrets of Race & Consciousness; Afrikan Cosmology of Kemet)*. Perhaps we can see how key this alignment is as the birth of the Sun Egg is taking place.

Metaphysical Key in Consciousness:

▲ Great Pyramid subterranean chamber of Geb and Nut

▲ The Divine Union/Embrace and Marriage of Geb and Nut

▲ Heaven Above and Heaven on Earth Below

Specifically, we turn our attention to the Great Pyramid, which reveals the subterranean chamber of Geb and Nut, indicated by the arrow, as pictured below and on the following page:

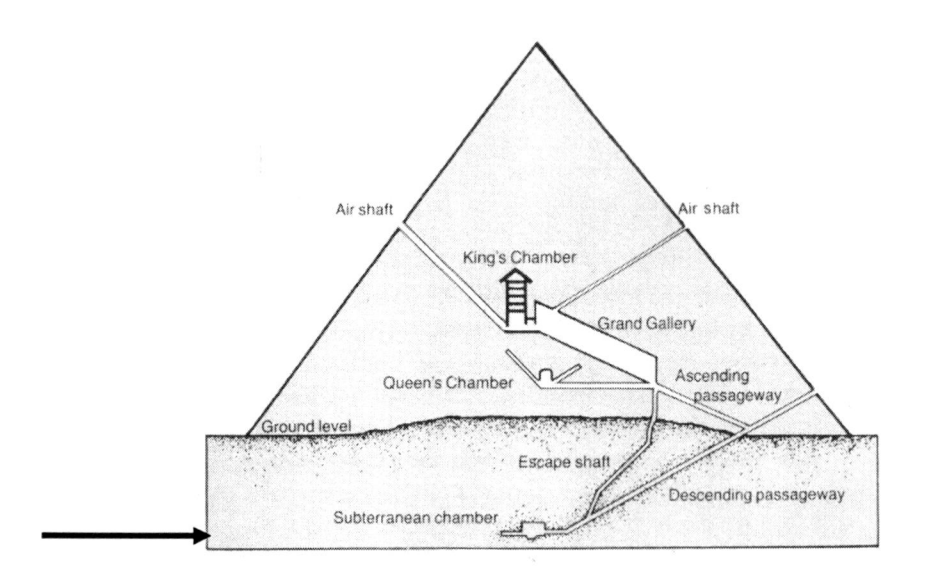

Notice Heru and Ausar/Auset at the apexes of the double Pyramids, and thus there is Heaven Above and Heaven on Earth Below, as pictured in the diagrams as follows:

Heaven Above

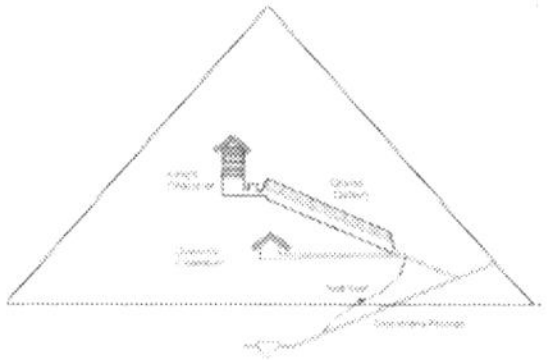

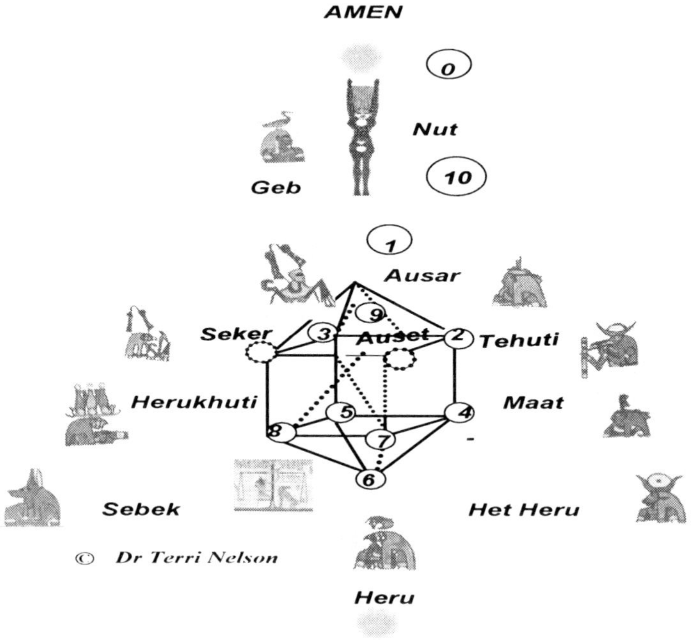

AMEN

(0)

Nut

Geb (10)

(1)
Ausar

Seker (9) (3) **Auset** (2) **Tehuti**

Herukhuti (8) (5) (4) **Maat**

(7)

(6)

Sebek **Het Heru**

© *Dr Terri Nelson*

Heru

Heaven on Earth

Below

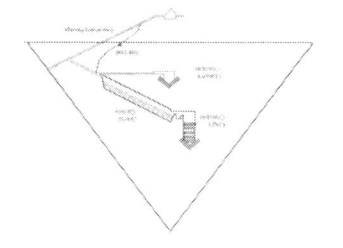

Metaphysical Key in Consciousness:

▲ When the Sun has been brought to Earth then as Heru we are able to affirm Nuk Ausar, Nuk Auset

When the Sun has been brought to Earth then as Heru we are able to affirm Nuk Ausar, Nuk Auset, I am Ausar, I am Auset, my Father, my Mother and I are One. This is biblically expressed as, my Father and I are One, which is but a half truth. When. Kemetically understood we see that Ausar and Auset are One.

Metaphysical Key in Consciousness:

▲Union/juncture between AusetAusar or KaBa and the Taut/Underword

We learn from *The Gods of the Egyptians VI* that the seeming union or juncture between Auset and Ausar or Ka and Ba is the personification of the Tuat or underworld described as "a narrow circular valley which begins where the sun sets in the West, and ends where he rises in the East" (172). As Auset and Ausar embrace they form a united body pictured on the following page. As we will see later, this is the junction of the new moon, where we move from total absence of light to first glimmer of new light. This is the point of moving from the tomb of seeming 'death' to the womb of rebirth.

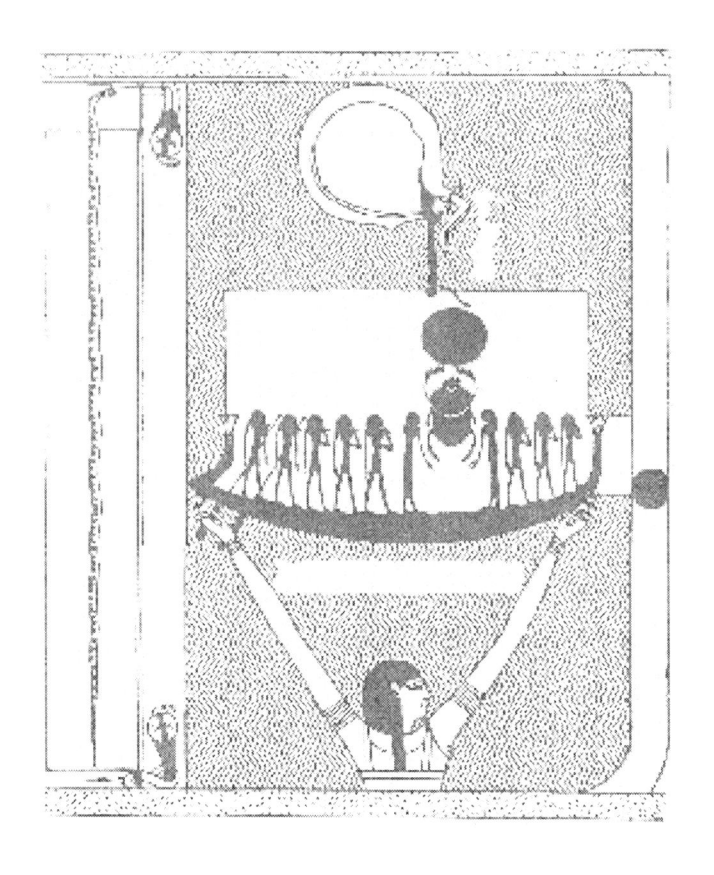

In this circular bending back, Auset and Ausar embrace, forming one united body. We see the Goddess Nut on the top of [their heads as: Ka/Ba, Ausar/Auset are at One] who supports with both hands the disk of the Sun. This is also pictured on the page that follows:

Dr Nteri Nelson　　　　Nteri Renenet Elson

Neteru revealing Harvest to the Sons and Daughters of God

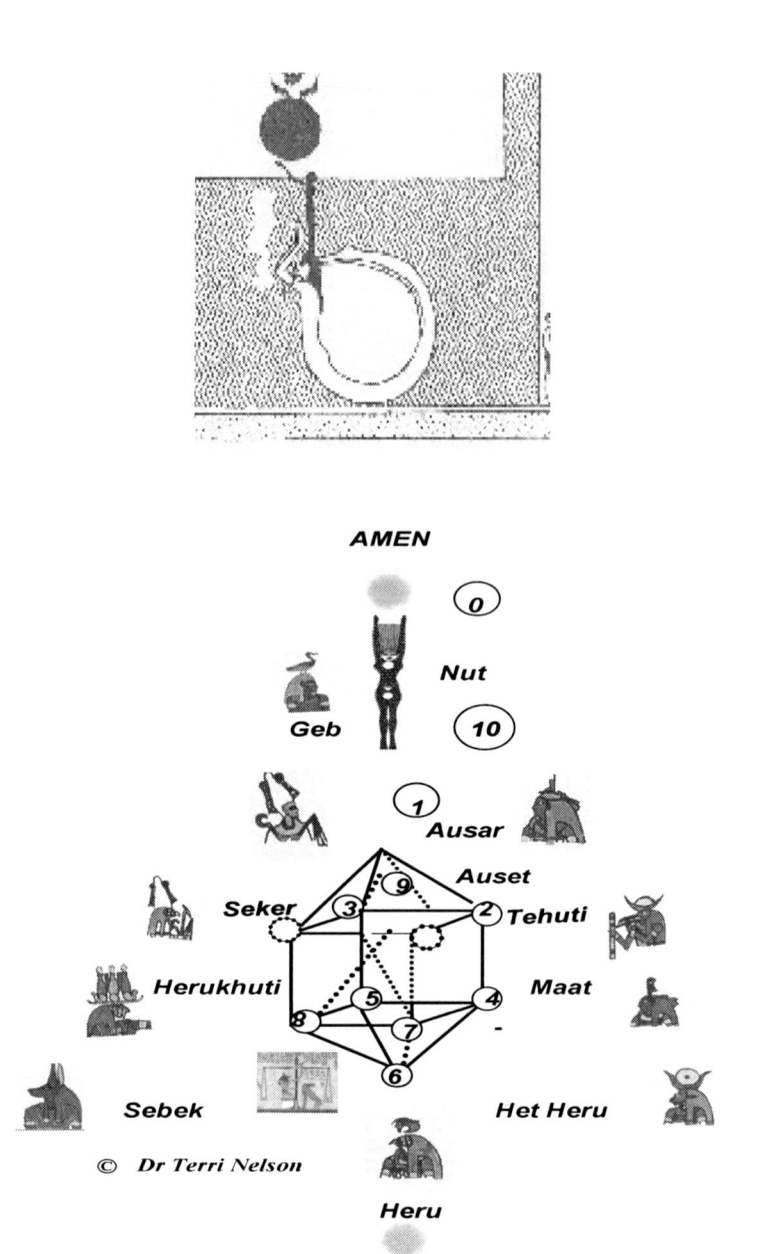

AMEN

© Dr Terri Nelson

Chapter 3

Metaphysical Key in Consciousness:

▲ The MerKaBa, *that is* the Tree of Life, that is the Great Pyramid MerAkhutu

Revealed is:

As the Tree of Life fully bends back upon itself, what we see next is that the following emerges:

- 2 more spheres, directly opposite

sphere 2 Tehuti/Djehuti and sphere 3 Seker and

- 2 veils or shrouds

Metaphysical Key in Consciousness:

▲ The Hidden Neteru Revealed

What is the meaning of these 2 hidden spheres/doors, on this plane? What Neteru are resident within these, as yet, unnumbered spheres, and indicated by the arrows in the diagram on the following page:

Dr Nteri Nelson   Nteri Renenet Elson

Neteru revealing Harvest to the Sons and Daughters of God

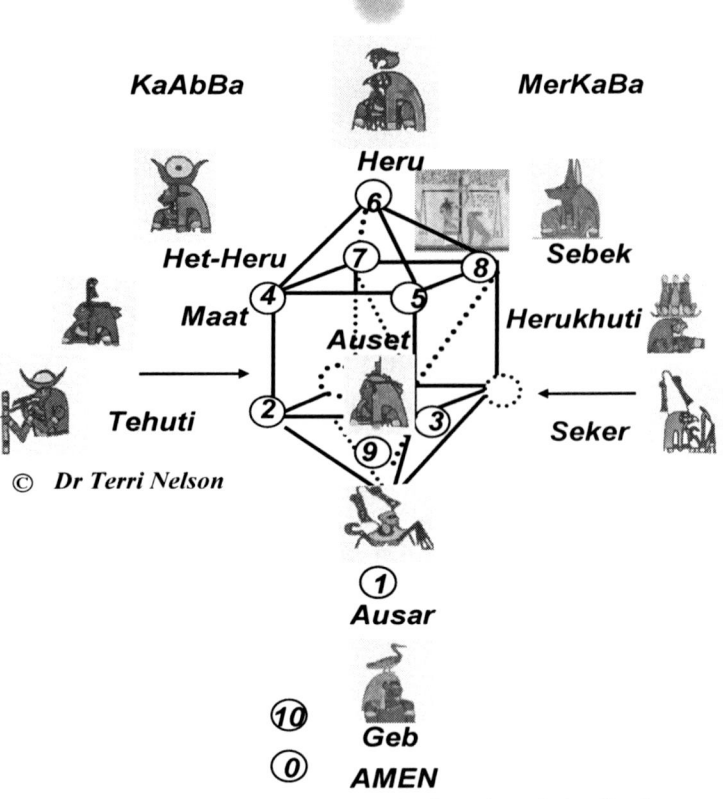

Tree of Life Great Pyramid MerAkhutu

KaAbBa   MerKaBa

Heru

Het-Heru   Sebek

Maat   Herukhuti

Auset

Tehuti   Seker

© *Dr Terri Nelson*

① Ausar

⑩ Geb

⓪ AMEN

Paut Neteru, Solar Bark, Chariot of the Gods

66

Metaphysical Key in Consciousness:

▲ The Hidden MerKaBa Tree of Life Neteru Revealed

What is revealed is that they are Nit (Neith) and Khnemu (Khnum). These Neteru reveal the *New* Tree of Life and that which was hidden in the MerKaBa.

Nit (Net, Ntr, Neith)

Khnemu (Khnum)

> Metaphysical Key in Consciousness:

▲ The 'New' Tree of Life MerKaBa Revealed

These Neteru are pictured in the MerKaBa below and in the linear Tree of Life on the next two pages.

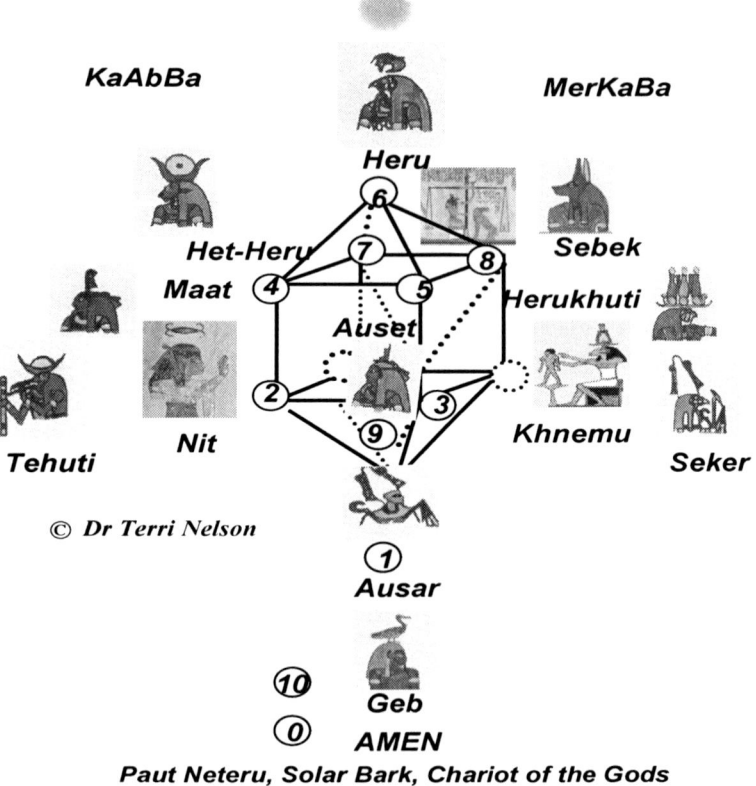

Tree of Life Great Pyramid MerAkhutu

Paut Neteru, Solar Bark, Chariot of the Gods

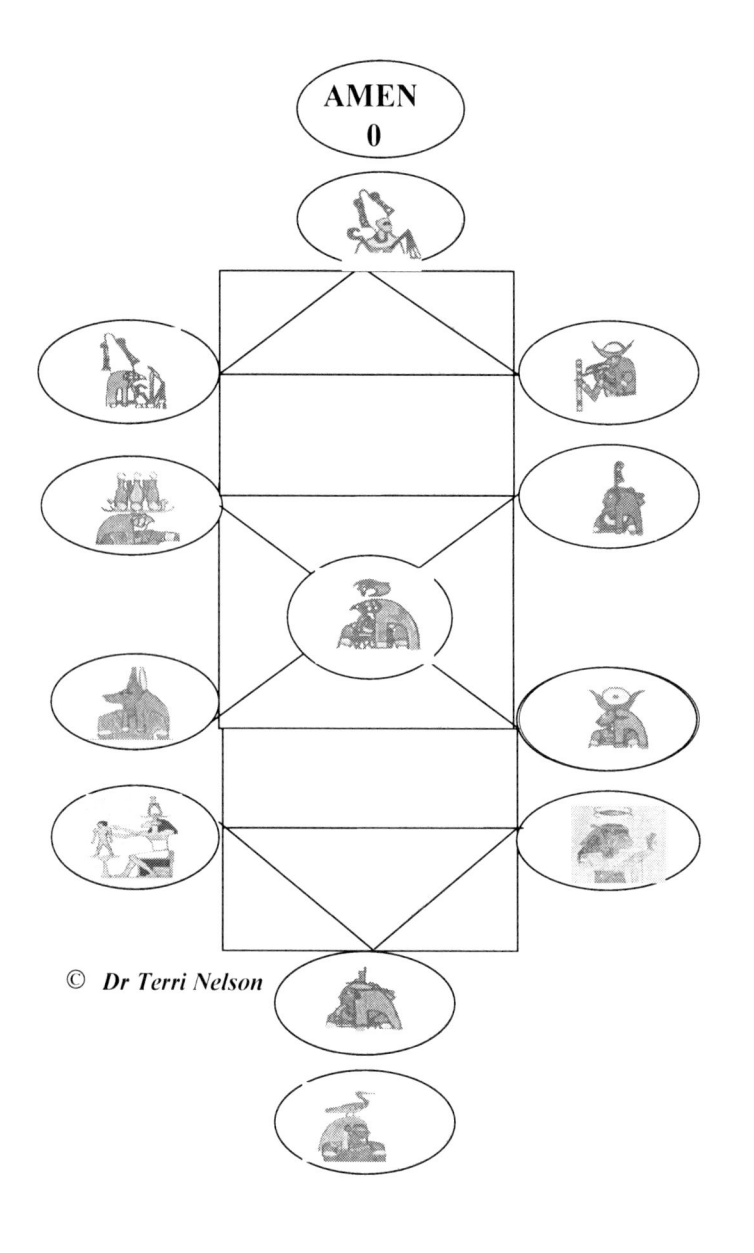

© Dr Terri Nelson

Neteru revealing Harvest to the Sons and Daughters of God

© *Dr Terri Nelson*

> Metaphysical Key in Consciousness:

▲ The Neter Nit or Net, Nrt, Neith

Indications of the Neter Nit or Net, Nrt, Neith were given in the book, *KaAbBa Building The Lighted Temple and the Metaphysical Keys to the Tree of Life,* on pages 172 -175.

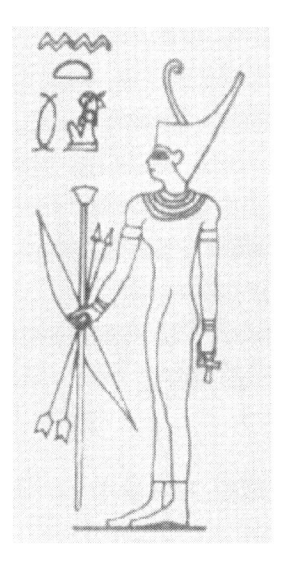

or

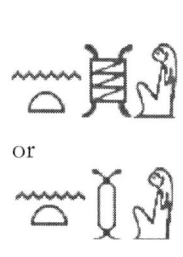

Neter Nit or Net, Nrt, Neith is One of the oldest Kemetic Neteru, dating back to predynastic times. She is pictured with various symbols which include in her hand; an ankh, two arrows, a bow, a sceptre, and upon her head; the red crown of the North and a shuttle.

Nit, or Neith is considered a 'Great Mother' and is synonymous with the Neteru Auset, Het-Heru and Nun. Her name means 'to knit or weave.' She is associated with: the power of protection, the power to conceive and bring forth the new Sun god daily, the feast of Lamps, and the power of the eye of Heru. Accordingly: E.A. Wallis Budge. *The Gods of the Egyptians, V.I,* p. 458 - 62:

> Nit, Net, the mighty mother, who had given birth to Ra, and that she was the first to give birth to anything, and that she had done so when nothing else had been born, and that she had never herself been born...the Being who was eternal and infinite, and was the creative and ruling power of heaven, earth, and the underworld, and of every creature and thing in them....

> Hail, mother great, not has been uncovered your birth! Hail, goddess great, within the underworld which is doubly hidden, you unknown one? Hail, you divine one great, not has been unloosed of your garment! O unloose your garment. Hail Hapt (Hidden one), not is given my way of entrance to her, come, receive you the soul of Ausar, protect it within [your] two hands...

The petition refers very distinctly to the mysterious character of the births of Net, and to her attribute of inscrutability in the **doubly hidden underworld,** and while the deceased declares that none has ever penetrated the cloak wherewith she is shrouded, he beseeches her to unloose it for him.

We learn further that Net is also regarded as the female counterpart of the ram headed Khnemu, known as the Neter of the First Cataract. He and his female counterpart have many similarities, as we will soon see.

462 continued:

... and an ancient legend declared that she arrayed Ausar in the apparel which had been specially woven for him by the two rekhti goddesses, i.e., Auset and Nephtys. And because of the part which she had taken in arraying Ausar in his graveclothes Net/Nit was made to preside over the "good house," i.e., the chamber in which the dead were embalmed and swathed in linen, and over the chambers of the temples in which the unguents which were employed in public worship were compounded. The unguents which she mixed for Ausar proved to be the means by which the body of the god was preserved from destruction and made young again, and happy were the dead who were able to secure the ministrations of Net/Nit.

Knits, knit, K(a) nit

Definition:

To make a fabric or garment by intertwining yard or thread in a series of connected loops either by hand with knitting needles or on a machine. 2. To become securely joined or mended together closely.

Nits, nit,

Definition:

Nit 1 – The egg or young of a parasitic insect, such as a louse.

Nit 2 – A unit of illuminative brightness equal to one candle per square meter, measured perpendicular to the rays of the source. [From Latin *nitor*, brightness, from *nitere*, to shine.] Please take note here of the Latin word *Nitere* and how this word dispelled reveals the word Neteri, Neter.

Meaning:

The name Net or Ent, spelled backwards is also a root for the word entity. It is Neter Nit or Net, Nrt, Neith that begins the entification process, or the coming into being (ness). Also, Nrt or enter(ing) into being. On a higher turn of the spiral, you are K(a) – Nit-ing together the garment of God. These Lighted 'Nits' are the many *sightings* of the 'self' now *seamlessly strung together* and realized as the *One and Only SELF.*

On a lower turn of the spiral these are the 'nits' that we become encapsulated and strangulated within as we see and falsely identify *self (and others)* as separate. This can leave us bereft of the fire, life and blood of Ra, and relying on the life blood of others. As we Build The Lighted Temple, we choose whether we are radiating Light energy or whether as louse we are blood draining. The Kemetic Goddess/Neter Nit (K-nit) weaves the threads of Light which are the garment of God. The cohering power of her love holds the garment together and her unguents make it 'sweet smelling' lest it fall apart, decay, be full of darkness, become extremely offensive and 'stink'. As we will see later, she has correspondence with the Neter Tehuti in the underlying unity in creation, 'individuated' as the Khus, divine intelligences or divine qualities.

> Metaphysical Key in Consciousness:

▲ Ka-Ra-acter or Ka-erect-er Building

▲ Ausarian Spiritual Transformation and Resurrection

▲ Ausar-ian Consciousness – ASTR

What's The Matter With Our Lives?

What's the matter with our lives is our density, coarseness, and lower vibration. You will overcome your descent into matter and begin your re-ascent into Spirit by clearing up the matter(s) within your own vehicles. In Ausarian Spiritual Transformation and Resurrection you are striving to be resurrected in Ausar-ian Consciousness – ASTR.

Within this acronym is another which is AST. AST is the another name for Auset. Ast and Ausar are synonymous with Ka and Ba. Likewise, Ast and Ausar and Ka and Ba are inseparable. ASTR, or the STAR Heru within you, is doing the work to raise your vibration by transmuting (changing) the sub-stance of your vehicles from a more dense, coarse material nature, which has a lower vibration, into a more refined and luminous solar substance of a higher vibration. This is the luminous MerKaBa body of Light.

When someone is told that they have a Ka-Ra-acter or Ka-erect-er that 'stinks' or is 'lousy' they are being told that they are reflecting a more 'materialized' Ka-Ra-acter which falls short in its approximation to the in-Spiriting Ka, the true Image and Likeness of God in which we are made. As the Initiate moves through the Halls of Amenta he or she beseeches the Neteru/Gods that his/her name is not made to 'stink'. This is expressed accordingly: E.A. Wallis Budge. *The Prt Em Hru. (The Egyptian Book Of The Dead),* p. 258, Chapter xxxb.

> Ausar, the scribe Ani, saith: "My heart my mother, my heart my mother, my heart my coming into being! May there be nothing to resist me at [my] judgment; may there be no opposition to me from the Tchatcha. May there be no parting of thee from me in the presence of him who keepeth the scales!
>
> **Thou art my Ka within my body [which] knitteth** and strengtheneth my limbs. Mayest thou come forth to the place of happiness to which I am advancing. **May the Shenit not cause my name to stink**, and may no lies be spoken against me in the presence of the god. Good is it for thee to hear.

Let's dispell the word Shenit:

t   S   h
e   i
    n

t / S   h
  / e   i
    n

 **Definition:**

<u>Shenit –</u>

A class of divine beings. E. A. Wallis Budge. *Prt Em Hru. (The Egyptian Book of The Dead)*, p. 258. May the Shenit, who make men to stand fast… Ibid. p. 309

Special ministers to the king, officials of the Court of Ausar. (*Osiris and the Egyptian Resurrection, V.1*), p. 333.

Those who have moved further along the path may be detected by their fragrant odour or aroma, having burnt off the dross of dense matter. Ka-erect-er/Ka-Ra-acter and personality speak to the quality, structure, function, fragrance, luminescence and purity of the instrument through which the Soul may operate and do its work in the World.

Ka-erect-er development is at work within your Spiritual equipment. As such, your Ka-Ra-acter is expressing itself through who you are and who you are becoming. Through your Ka-Ra-acter, others are able to see how Ra is in action upon the stage of life as the *emerging* Sun (Son/Daughter) of God in you.

Ka-erect-er is built or 'erected. *It is the blended essence or bouquet of fragrant qualities* that arise once the personality structure is blended, coordinated and balanced. After even a partial dispelling of the word Ka-Ra-acter, the vital importance of its development can not be overemphasized in the Spiritual Journey of unfolding consciousness and Ausarian Resurrection.

You can not get where you think you are going without great moral Ka-erect-er. This is why the Manes in his/her prayers to the Gods beseeches them *'not to make his/her Name to Stink'*. (Refer to page 172 of, *KaAbBa Building The Lighted Temple and the Metaphysical Keys to the Tree of Life,* for *Ritual* verse from, *The Prt Em Hru (The Egyptian Book Of The Dead)*. The Lotus petals unfold as Ka-Ra-acter is developed. The story of Ausar and Auset reveals insight into the meaning of:

1. Scent or odour of Ka-Ra-acter
2. Re-gaining immortality by passing through the purificatory fires in order to transmute the more coarse, material substance of your vehicles into a more refined, Solar substance.

> Metaphysical Key in Consciousness:

▲ The Neter Khnemu, Khnum

As mentioned, Nit is the female counterpart of the ram headed Khnemu. He is the next Neter to be revealed in the MerKaBa, Tree of Life. Here, he is seen seated and fashioning man(kind) upon the potter's wheel. He is sometimes pictured with Tehuti standing behind him.

Khnemu (Khnum)

Like Nit he too is one of the oldest Kemetic Neteru, dating back to predynastic times. Interestingly, he too carries the symbols of the scepter, ankh and wears the White Crown of the South, which is complimentary to his female counterpart's Red Crown of the North. Like the Nesut Bity (King) Narmer in uniting the land of Kemet, these combined crowns (described later) are the symbol of unification within us, a Kingdom which is both human and divine. Both are Neteru of the eleventh (11th) Hour of Night. Both have titles which describe them as the "Father of fathers, and Mother of mothers". Both Nit and Khnemu are self created, creating something-ness out of nothing-ness. They are at the beginingless beginning. Together they have a son named Tutu.

Just as his female counterpart Nit works with a shuttle, Khnemu works with a potter's wheel, both fashioning humankind. His name, likewise indicates a creative process and means to unite, join, build, which is expressed accordingly: E.A. Wallis Budge. *The Gods of the Egyptians, V2*, p. 50. [Khnemu]

> made the first egg from which sprang the sun, and he made the gods, and fashioned the first man upon a potter's wheel, and he continued to "build up" their bodies and maintain their life...

> The builder of men and the maker of the gods and the Father who was in the beginning, maker of things which are, creator of things which shall be, the source of things which exist, Father of fathers, and Mother of mothers, Father of the fathers of the gods and goddesses, lord of created

things from himself, maker of heaven and earth and the Tuat, and water and mountains.

In a long discourse with his governor, King Tcheser learns that Khnemu is the guardian of the flooding of the Nile which is expressed accordingly: E. A. Wallis Budge. *The Gods of The Egyptians, V.II,* p. 52 -54.

> He told him that the Nile flood came forth from the Island of Abu (Elephantine) whereon stood the first city that ever existed; out of it rose the Sun when he went forth to bestow life upon man, and therefore it is also called "Doubly Sweet Life,"…It was he [Khenemu] who kept the doors that held it in, and who drew back the bolts at the proper time…

King Tcheser further learns that while in the Delta of Kemet the Nile had only risen seven cubits which had contributed to a seven year drought, it had been rising to a height of twenty - eight cubits in Abu. To gain increase, King Tcheser then goes to make supplication to Khnemu, who appears before him and says,

> I am Khnemu the Creator. My hands rest upon you to protect your person, and to make sound your   body. I gave you your heart…I am he who created himself. I am the primeval watery abyss,

and I am Nile who riseth at his will…" Finally the Neter promised that the Nile should rise every year, as in olden time and described the good which should come upon the land when he had made an end of the famine.

The story continues as King Tcheser recounts that Khnemu had complained that his temple had been unkempt, in ruin and without sacrifice to the Neteru, whereupon, the King ordered the following decree:

> …certain lands on each side of the Nile near Abu [Elephantine] should be set apart for the endowment of the temple of Khnemu, and that a certain tax should be levied upon every product of the neighborhood and devoted to the maintenance of the priesthood of the Neter;

What happens next holds relevance to our current story of , *KaAbBa: The Great Pyramid is The Tree of Life: MerKaBa,* which is:

> …the original text of the decree was written upon wood, and as this was not lasting, the king ordered a copy of it should be cut upon a stone stele which should be set in a prominent place.

Metaphysical Key in Consciousness:

▲ Great Pyramid and the preservation of the Tree of Life: MerKaBa - in *stone*.

Our ancestor Nesut Bity Tcheser gives us the notion that an important decree, such as this, must be set in stone to have permanence, and not in wood. Metaphysically, the Tree of Life is a symbol, whose replica(tion) has made it and its most valued knowledge 'transportable' out of Kemet. Physically, the tree of life is made of wood. Yet here, by analogy, has not its decree likewise, been made in stone, to give it physical permanency? Stated again, the purpose of this Capstone book is to have us look *within* the Great Pyramid itself for the preservation of the Tree of Life: MerKaBa - in *stone*.

Metaphysical Key in Consciousness:

▲Nit and Khnemu correlated with the energies of Tehuti and Seker.

Just opposite Khnemu in the KaAbBa MerKaBa, Great Pyramid and Tree of Life is Sphere 3, Seker. This sphere has correspondence with Ptah and is referred to at times as Ptah Seker. Likewise, just opposite the Neter Nit (Neith) we find Sphere 2 Tehuti. A reciprocal role in the creative process is going on between these 4 spheres and is hinted at accordingly: E. A. Wallis Budge. *The Gods of The Egyptians, V.II,* p. 502.

> Ptah [read here: Seker/Ptah] was the fellow-worker with Khnemu in carrying into effect the commands concerning the creation of the universe which were issued by Tehuti, and while the latter was engaged in fashioning man and animals, the former was employed in the construction of the heavens and the earth.

More will be given in a subsequent Volume of this work regarding the relationship between all the spheres in the Tree of Life and these newly revealed spheres in,

KaAbBa: The Great Pyramid is The Tree of Life: MerKaBa.

For now, we are told that Nit and Khnemu are highly correlated with the energies of Tehuti and Seker. And why would this not be so, given the 'mirroring' between AusetAusar, KaBa, MotherFather as seen in the following diagram:

Neteru revealing Harvest to the Sons and Daughters of God

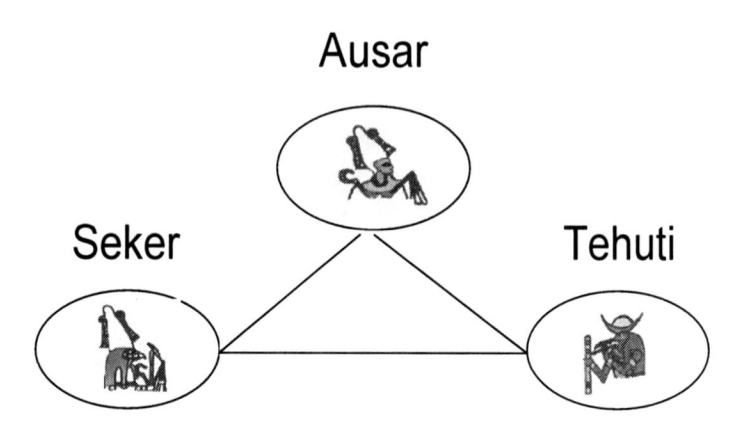

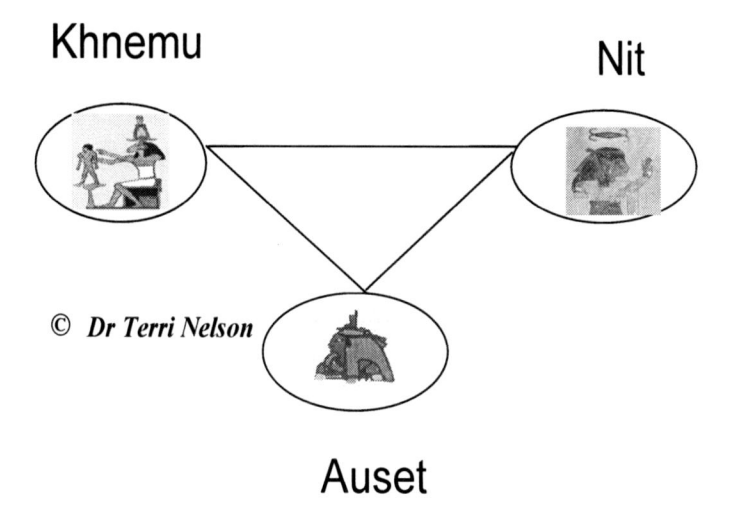

> Metaphysical Key in Consciousness:

▲ Sphere 2 Tehuti/Djehuti. Sphere 3, Seker

▲ Ka Ab Ba Building The Lighted Temple

Suffice it for now to note that in the Book, *KaAbBa Building The Lighted Temple and the Metaphysical Keys to the Tree of Life,* we may recall that we are using these aspects of our Spiritual faculty to access qualities of energy that may be used positively/skillfully, at their optimal, divine expression or negatively/unskillfully at their most inharmonious expression. So the resonance and correspondence with Nit and Khnemu respectively may be sensed and seen within the qualities of energy for Tehuti and Seker respectively, and are restated here as follows:

> **Metaphysical Key To:**
> Sphere 2 Tehuti Neterological Energy

Planets: Neptune (Jupiter)

Signs: Pisces (Sagittarius)

+ Positive Qualities/ Skilled Use

•Divine Ideation & archetypes In The Mind Of God

The Divine Khus

•Divine Wisdom

•Supreme Intelligence

•Divine Mind

•Divine Love

•Truth

•Unity Underlying Diversity

•The Whole Moving Geometrical Arrangement In The Mind Of God

•The Divine Box Cover Of The Multitudinous Piece Puzzle of Creation

•Knowledge Of Whole, Part And Perfect Relationship Between

•Unity As The Perfect Idea In The Mind Of God

•Intuition

•Divinely Intended Architectural Design And Plan for Manifestation - Pure And Perfect Without Distortion Or Flaw

•Light & Illumination

•Dissolver of Boundaries

•Omniscience

•Resolver of 'Seeming' Duality Into The One

•Synthesizing Power Of Love And Wisdom Cohering The Myriad Particularizations Or Pieces Of Created Forms Into The Seamless Unity Of The One

•Unity Underlying Diversity

•The Divine (oracle) Utterances That Bring Us To The Apex Of Any Triangle - A Point Of Resolution Into Light Supernal

•Expanse Into Wholeness, Oneness, and Unity With All Beings

- *Negative Qualities/Unskilled Use*

•Tapping into Limited Circumscribed Contents of Concrete Mind to Solve Life's Problems Without Reference with Divinely Intended Archetypal Design

---

Metaphysical Key To:

Sphere 3 Seker Neterological Energy

Planet: Saturn

Signs: Capricorn (Aquarius)

+ Positive Qualities/ Skilled Use

•Creative Power & intelligence

•Vibrational drawing of the circle which contains the greatest good

•'Ring Pass Not' or Circumscribed Field of Experience in which Divine Purpose is to be Structured and Made Manifest.

•The Authoritative Demand for the Full Vibrational Sounding and Expression of the One True SELF in the to-be Manifested Form

•Creates Structure and Sets Limits within which Full Creative Potential is to be Expressed

•Exacting, Efficient, Effective, Capable, Fully Equipped, Achieving the Goal of the Archetypal Design

•Vibrational Sounding of the to-be Created Forms Fostering Evolutionary Process

•Infinite Potential in a Vibrationaly Drawn Boundaried Field of Expression

•Words of Power, Hekau,

•Alloter of the to-be 'Ringed' (boundaried) Space/time Cyclical Schedule •The Power in Achieving One's Intended Purpose in Fullness Through Graduated 'Ring-Pass-Nots' of Boundaried Experiences

- Negative Qualities/Unskilled Use

•Harsh Over Demanding or, Weak Under Demanding Father, Authority

•Ineffectual, Impotent, Incompetent

•Unable to Set or Hold Structural Limits for Self Unfoldment and Manifestation

•Lack of Structure or Authority

•Rigidity or Crystallization of Structure

•Unbridled Power and Abuse

•Creates New Form or Destroys/Shatters Old Form Indiscriminately/Prematurely

• Undisciplined

Metaphysical Key in Consciousness:

▲ Worlds Built with and without Nit and Khnemu

We might then ask the question: What has it meant for the building of this World without the conscious awareness of the Neteru Nit and Khnemu in the MerKaBa Tree of Life?

Absent the precision of these Neteru, their adherence to the light and complimentary with Seker and Tehuti, could this account for why this world is built askew the divinely intended design or out of whack. Could this account for the grotesque creation of a separative, materialistic world?

Metaphysical Key in Consciousness:

▲ Spherical Luminous Body of Light

We are Spirit. In order to make an 'appearance' in the physical realm we need an instrument or equipment. Our physical, emotional and mental bodies are constructed for use from 7th, 6th, and 5th plane substance. When we live a 'linear consciousness' we can literally be focused from the waist down in these seeming lower planes of consciousness, unrefreshed by the Spiritual livingness of the 4th, 3rd, 2nd and 1st planes of consciousness, seemingly above.

Like an extremity cut off from its blood supply, the cutting off of our seemingly lower equipment from our seemingly higher equipment can cause the setting in of atrophy, decay, and death. As such, we lose sight of our circularity and spherical nature where All is in flow and we have to 'nit' ourselves back together again. As Knower, you are called to Build the Lighted Temple. The divine Image and Likeness is always present in you. More will be given on the 7 planes of consciousness later in this Capstone book (p. 118 -121).

We must move with the awareness that we are Spirit even if that Spirit does not as yet don the (finest) form or vesture. We do the work to purify the material form substance or vestitures enough to see, capture and reflect this image. You often hear talk of folks wanting the 'finest robes' or outfits. We feel that if we dress in the best finery it will reveal something of the quality of who we are. In reality, your best 'threads' are spun with a super atomic sub-stance *so fine* that scientists are still trying to figure out how to 'see' and 'identify' this spherical, luminous body of Light. As Heru, Sun-Son/Daughter let us affirm that: I have bent over backwards in my quest to be as , the One True Self.

Metaphysical Key in Consciousness:

▲Beyond hierarchical and linear consciousness the Luminous Spiritual body of Spherical Consciousness.
▲MerKaBa - Mer(ror)/mirror, the image and likeness of the Neteru God

Ka and Ba, Ausar and Auset, Father and Mother are in embrace within you. As this becomes so, you move beyond a hierarchical and linear consciousness view of yourself into the luminous Spiritual body of spherical consciousness. We see more clearly in the Mer(ror) or mirror, the image and likeness of the Neteru God that we are.

In Metu Neter the symbol of the chisel has the sounds of both ab (ib) and mer. It is in the temple building that we chisel the monument of ourselves. This is pictured below and on the next two pages:

Notice Geb and Nut below and forming the cross bar of the Merror above. To be as Heru, one must follow the narrow middle or razor edge path.

Dr Nteri Nelson   **Nteri Renenet Elson**

Neteru revealing Harvest to the Sons and Daughters of God

© Dr Terri Nelson

KaAbBa: The Great Pyramid is The Tree of Life: MerKaBa

Secrets Revealed in The MerAkhutu

'Mirror, Mirror on the wall am I nearest to the All?

KaAbBa: The Great Pyramid is The Tree of Life: MerKaBa

Metaphysical Key in Consciousness:

▲ The MerKaBa Neteru Tools of Creation

▲ Shuttle, Bow, Arrows, Potter's Wheel

Nit weaves the little light 'nits' together. These supper atomic particles are like the tiniest of 'bubbles'. Similar to a child blowing long strings of bubbles, she is breathing forth strings of bubbly Light that will become the filaments which her husband Khnemu will use to fashion man/woman and pictured on the following page:

Her bow and arrow weapons are used in the warfare of maintaining the highest Light. If a bubble or lighted nit is ill formed, she draws forth her arrow on her bow, takes aims and shoots her arrow, so that no-thing that is unrepresentative of the Light of the Neteru, God is allowed to come into manifestation. If necessary, she draws doubly upon her bow, in this swift process, as the instant the light nit is blown forth it can be shaped, concretized and made manifest.

They must be perfect before they can be received by her husband on his potter's wheel who then gives them the earthly 'dust' element of densification. Here we have 'heaven' and 'earth' coming together. Consorts Nit and Khnemu are working together, just as Nut and Geb.

There is no right or left brain dominance that would hold her shuttle or wand in one or the other hand. Instead this is a tool of balanced precision handled from all sides by the unitive, all seeing eye of Nit as she provides the sheerest, most luminous garment of entification in the creation process. Nit and Knemu are entification and densification working hand and hand. Working in correspondence with the Tehuti and Seker, in the underlying unity in creation, Nit and Khnemu give 'individuated' livingness, to the Khus, so that divine intelligences or divine qualities are tangibly expressed.

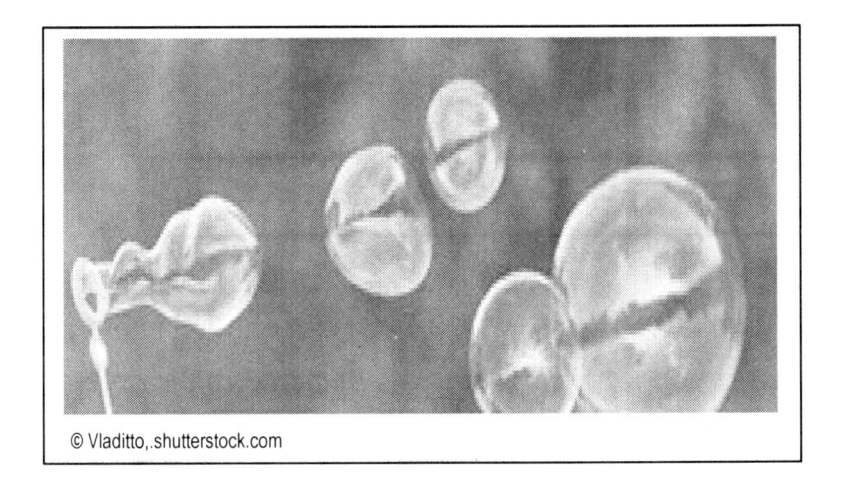

© Vladitto,.shutterstock.com

In his correspondence with the astrological sign of Aquarius, the bearer of the 'Spiritual' waters, Khnemu opens the gates, bearing the waters of the Nile, or Hapi River. The symbol of the earthen vessel in his name is shown below:

In her correspondence with the astrological signs of Cancer and Virgo, Nit bears a shuttle, symbol of generativity and precision, also in her name and shown below:

> Metaphysical Key in Consciousness:

▲ The Uniting of the North and South, the Red and White Crown

In a Hymn to Ausar, reference is made to the crowns in the *Prt Em Hru. The Book of Coming Forth By Day* by E. A Wallis Budge accordingly:

Hymn to Ausar

> "Glory be to Ausar Un-nefer, ...lord of the
> crowns of the North and South, lord of the lofty
> white crown. Exalted Being. Homage to thee,
> King of kings, Lord of Lords, Prince of
> princes..."

Pictured here is Nesut Bity Narmer, or Menes who was
ruler of Kemet around 3100 B.C.E. He united the North
and the South of Kemet and was the first man recorded
wearing the crown of unification.

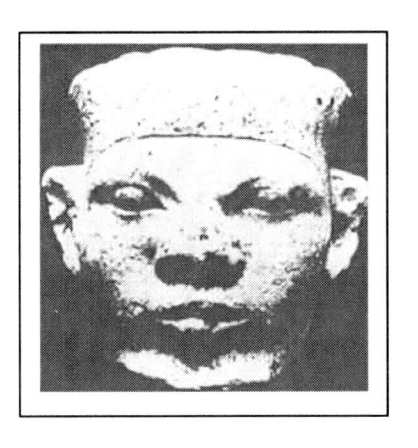

We derive knowledge of these crowns from the
Narmer (Menes) Palette; front-side/left and obverse-
side/right are pictured on the next page. Notice the
white crown the King is wearing in the palette front-
side at left and the red crown the King is wearing in
the palette obverse- side at right, as indicated by the
arrows.

Dr Nteri Nelson   Nteri Renenet Elson

Neteru revealing Harvest to the Sons and Daughters of God

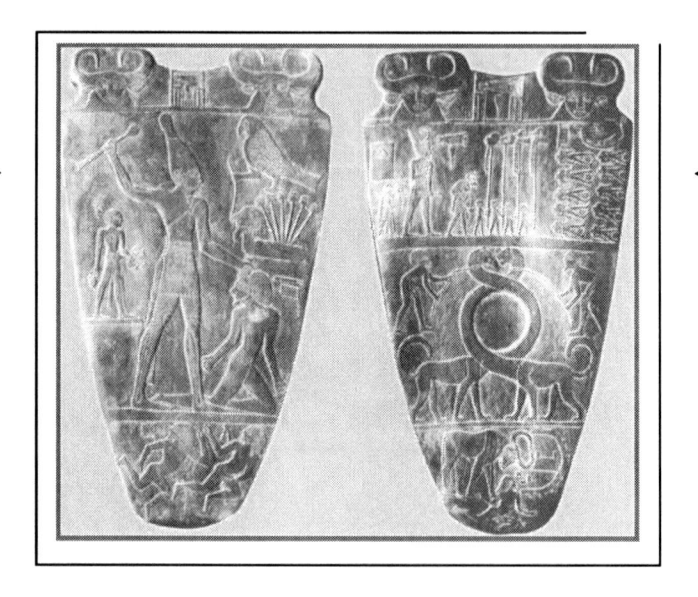

Crown 1 - is called the Hedjet, the White Crown of the South and worn by the ruler King of Upper Kemet.

Crown 2 - is called Deshret, the Red crown of the North and worn by the ruler King of Lower Kemet.

Crown 3 - is called the Pschent. It is the combination of crown 1 and 2 and is worn by the ruler King who has unified the North and the South of Kemet. This Double crown of Ancient Kemet. is referred to as Sekhemti, the Two Powerful Ones.

Heru, the son of Ausar and Auset is pictured wearing the Double Crown of Kemet.

Metaphysical Key in Consciousness:

▲ The Mesu Heru 4 Sons of Heru Above and Below

Like the 4 Mesu Heru (sons of Heru) represented as spheres 4 Ma'at, 5 Herukhuti, 7 Het-Heru and 8 Sebek Above, we also see the Mesu Heru Below represented as sphere 2 Tehuti, sphere 3 Seker, sphere (unnumbered) Nit, sphere (unnumbered) Khneumu.

Metaphysical Key in Consciousness:

▲ The Crowning and Seating of the King Heru upon his/her Throne, as heir of Ausar and Auset. As Heru, you have united the seeming duality of Ka and Ba, of

Mother Auset and Father Ausar, of Matter and Spirit within your Constitution which is both human and divine. This is the crowning and seating of Heru upon his/her throne as heir to the Kingdom. As the Sun-Son/Daughter, you are Divine 'Presence' on Earth. Not to be distorted as the material 'presents' at Christmas time at the so called birth of the son.

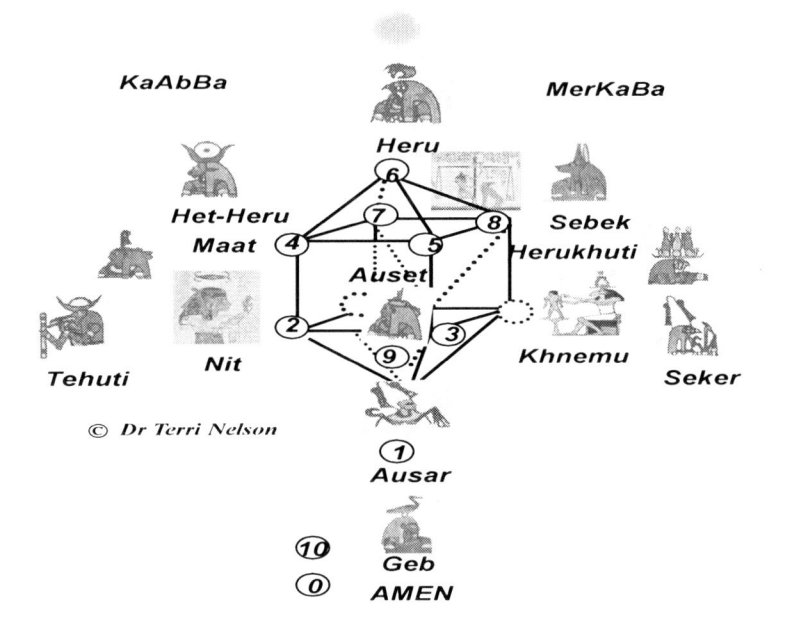

!!!See Appendix for important excerpts from:

Ausar, The Pope, Santa Claus, Christmas, and Christianity, **revealing more distortions on the crowns, etc. p. 130-158.**

Chapter 4

Metaphysical Key in Consciousness:

▲ The AUM

    A - Ausar

    U - Heru

    M - Auset

AUM I AM

As Heru sphere 6 in the Tree of Life, you are the Word, that re-becomes THE WORD in your long pilgrimage to reconstruct the broken body of Ausar.

Through the sounding of this powerful Hekau, (word of Power), the 'U' which saw duality, comes to see as One and affirms: 'I AM', the divine marriage between Ausar-sphere 1 and Auset-sphere 9, Father/Mother, Spirit/Matter. KaAbBa, MerKaBa, sees full circle. It is the eye of Heru, the All seeing eye, seen below, perched within the whole moving geometry within the mind of God:

1. You hold and see all within your Ab – heart.
2. You Mer (Mirror) the Image and Likeness of Father/Mother God – KaBa.

3. You become the Paut Neteru, Solar Bark or Chariot of Gods, MerKaBa.
4. You are now *impulsed from an effortless stream wherein the Will of God is known and* your co-creative Son/Daughter Sun-Ship is made manifest – *The Lighted Temple is Built.*

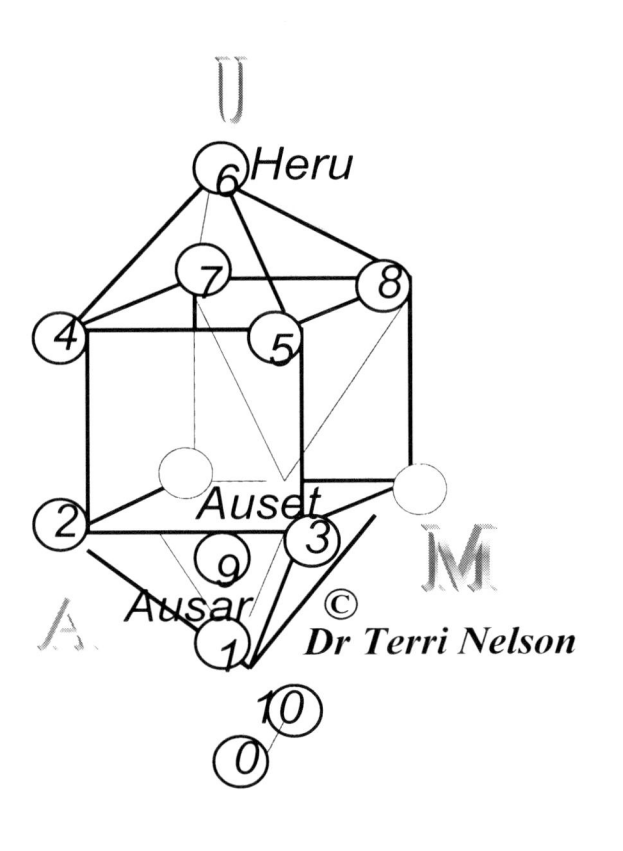

Neteru revealing Harvest to the Sons and Daughters of God

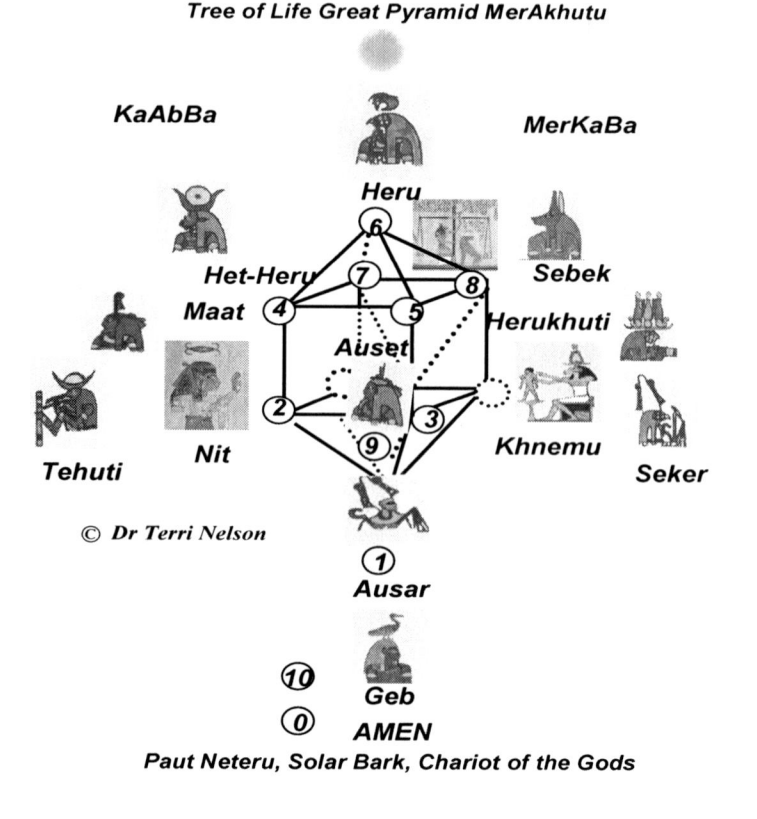

Tree of Life Great Pyramid MerAkhutu

KaAbBa

MerKaBa

Heru

Het-Heru

Maat

Sebek

Herukhuti

Auset

Nit

Khnemu

Tehuti

Seker

© *Dr Terri Nelson*

Ausar

Geb

AMEN

Paut Neteru, Solar Bark, Chariot of the Gods

Metaphysical Key in Consciousness:

▲ The MerKaBa Luminous Energy Body of Light
The MerKaBa is your luminous body of light. It is your energy body. Stepping into the awareness of this body is an awareness beyond just your physical body. It is the vehicle in which you have assess to all potential and unlimited supply. Again, within/as the luminous Lighted body you are impulsed from an effortless stream wherein the Will of the Neteru is known.

The MerKaBa is a luminous vehicle of:

> Rebirth, Transformation, Resurrection
>
> Ascension, Transport, Empowerment
>
> Enlightenment, Initiation, Service

The MerKaBa is a planisphere of the heavens. From within we are able to gaze the heavens, seeing the Neteru and the energies channeled through each constellation and planet for our enhancement, as pictured on the following page: You must visualize and move with/as the planisphere, within MerKaBa. There is a 'rounding' effect taking place, where all seeming squares, corners are made spherical in consciousness.

Metaphysical Key in Consciousness:

▲ The Planisphere of the Universe

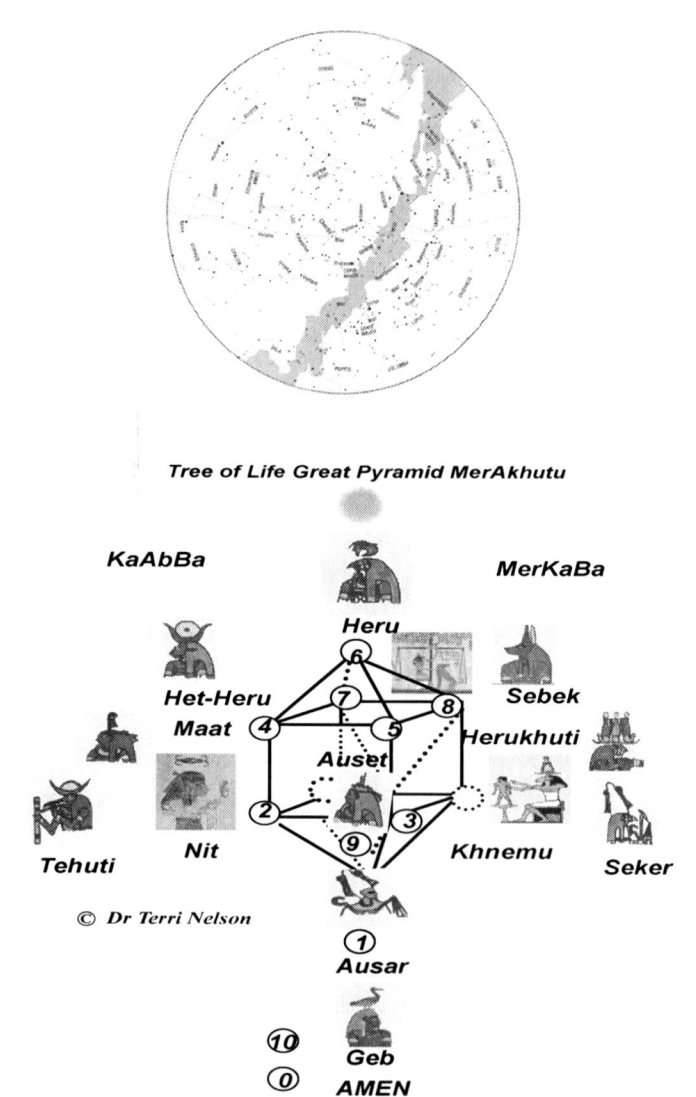

Tree of Life Great Pyramid MerAkhutu

KaAbBa   **MerKaBa**

Heru

Het-Heru   **Sebek**
Maat   **Herukhuti**

Auset

Tehuti   **Nit**   **Khnemu**   **Seker**

© *Dr Terri Nelson*

Ausar

Geb

AMEN

Paut Neteru, Solar Bark, Chariot of the Gods

KaAbBa: The Great Pyramid is The Tree of Life: MerKaBa
Secrets Revealed in The MerAkhutu

As Heru in the sign of Leo, may we as the Sun/Son-Daughter in the age of Aquarius, re-ascend in the sky above the Great MerAkhutu. May we bear witness that my Mother/Father/KaBa and I are One. Ka Ab Ba.

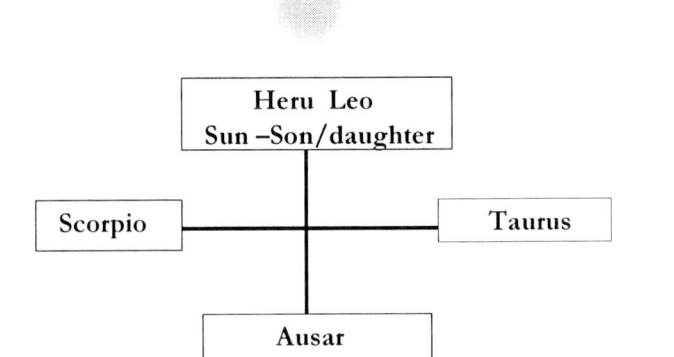

> Metaphysical Key in Consciousness:

▲Ka Ab Ba as seen Cosmically in the Sun - Earth - Moon cycles

We have learned that the meaning of the name Khnemu is to unite or join. We also learn, expressed accordingly: E. A. Wallis Budge. *The Gods of The Egyptians, V.II,* p. 50.

> ...astronomically the name refers to the "conjunction " of the sun and moon at stated seasons of the year...

In referring to the Book, *KaAbBa Building The Lighted Temple and the Metaphysical Keys to the Tree of Life,* p. 192 -195, the reader may review the cosmological conjunction as expressed through this alignment of:

- Ka Auset Moon

- Ba Ausar Sun

- Ab Heru Earth - Ascendant, Ab becomes the Sun/Son-Daughter

As mentioned, the Neteru Khnemu has resonance with the astrological sign Aquarius. Our reconnection with Khnemu and his counterpart Nit signal the dawning of the New Age of Aquarius, the eleventh sign in the Zodiac. He carries the water jug, and controls the door bolts on the Nile, bringing needed spiritual water to thirsty humanity, and cleansing and clearing away the rubble and debris of the cycle materialism. His name means to unite, and so we are moved from a separative consciousness into one of unity. He and Nit appear now in our 11th hour. Another mirroring at the hour when 1 and 1 are at One.

New Moon in Sun/Moon Cycle

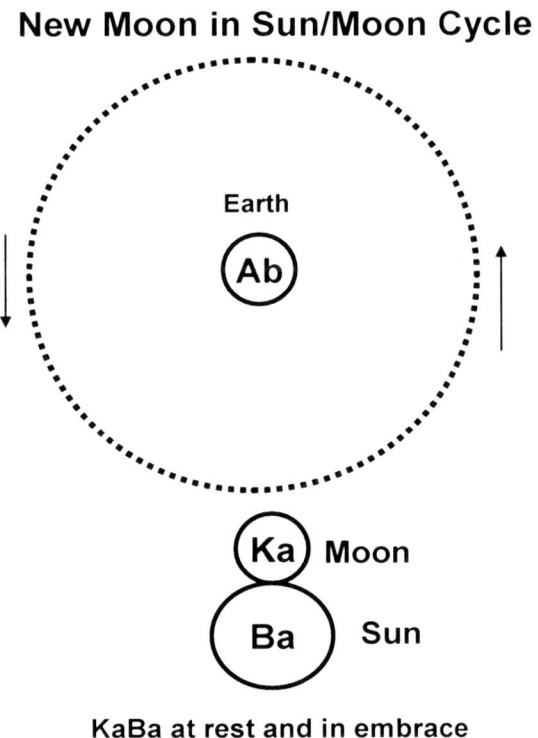

KaBa at rest and in embrace

0 degrees of separation
conjunction

© *Dr Terri Nelson*

Metaphysical Key in Consciousness:

▲ KaAbBa and Orion's Belt So Above So Below, So Below as Above

We may also see the correspondence in KaAbBa and Orion's Belt. Again, so above so below, so below as above. That which is happening in the Spiritual journey of unfolding consciousness in humanity on Earth is reflected in the story of the stars or the stellar myths. This is shown in the diagrams on the next three pages:

KaAbBa: The Great Pyramid is The Tree of Life: MerKaBa
Secrets Revealed in The MerAkhutu

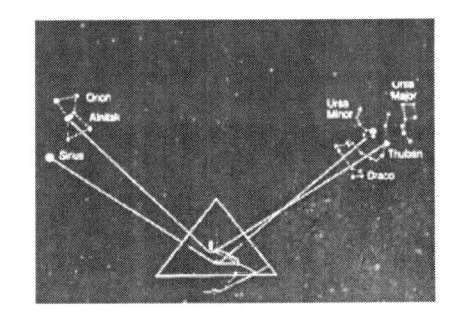

crystalinks.com

Ka

Ab

Ba

Neteru revealing Harvest to the Sons and Daughters of God

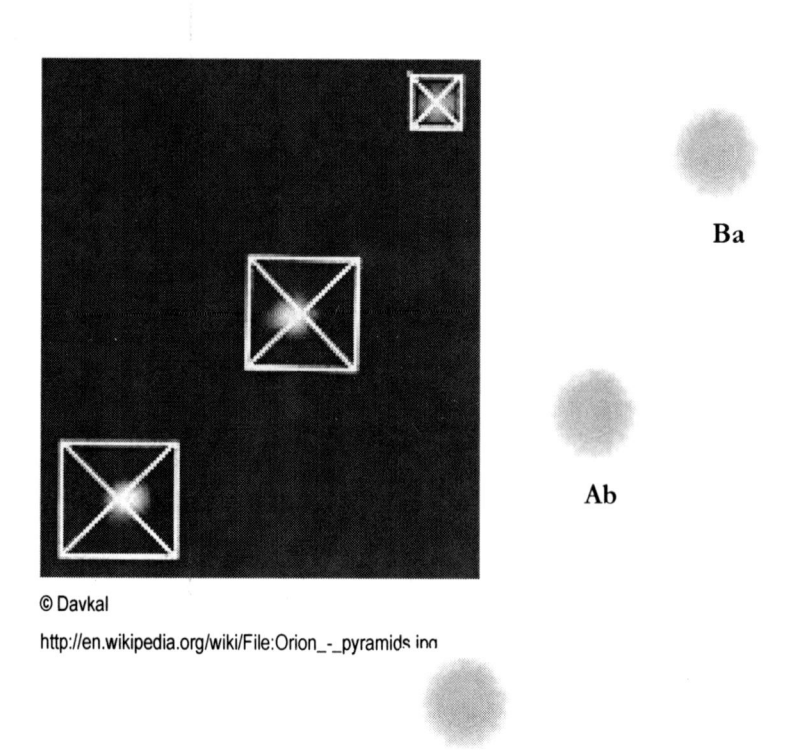

Ba

Ab

Ka

KaAbBa: The Great Pyramid is The Tree of Life: MerKaBa

Secrets Revealed in The MerAkhutu

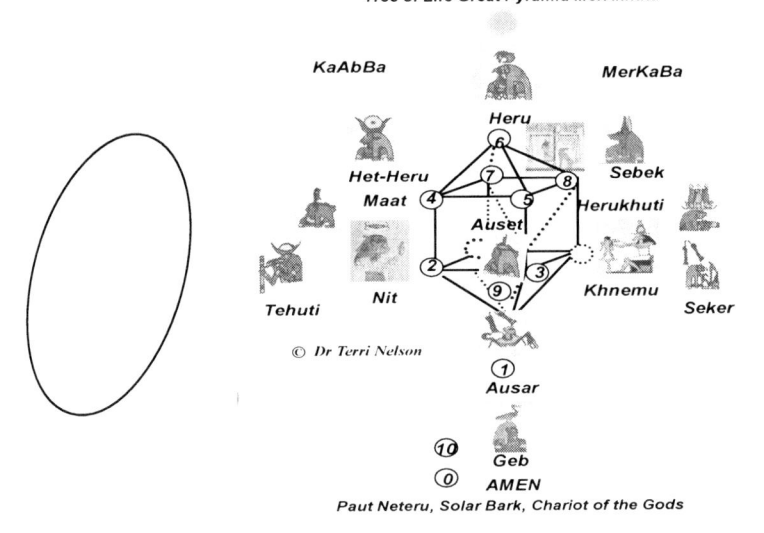

Tree of Life Great Pyramid MerAkhutu

KaAbBa

MerKaBa

Heru

Het-Heru

Maat ④

Sebek

Herukhuti

Auset

Tehuti

Nit

Khnemu

Seker

© Dr Terri Nelson

① Ausar

⑩

⓪

Geb

AMEN

Paut Neteru, Solar Bark, Chariot of the Gods

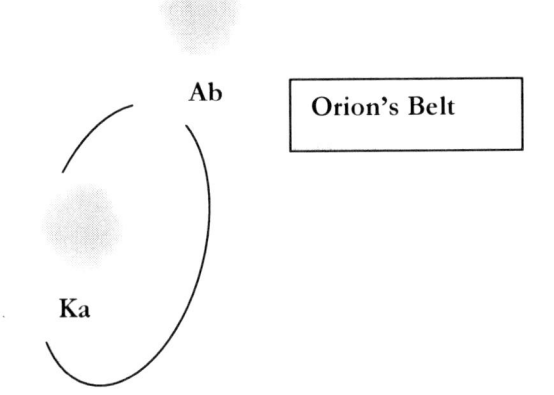

Ab

Orion's Belt

Ka

Ba

> Metaphysical Key in Consciousness:

▲The Secret Chamber, which is the Tomb and the Womb of rebirth. The Secret Chamber of the Tomb and the Womb are revealed in the MerKaBa.

▲The 2 and 4 Veils or Shrouds

▲The doubly hidden underworld

This Chamber is veiled, shrouded on all 4 sides. One veil has likewise kept hidden the Neter Nit and Neter Khnemu in the Tree of Life as shown on the following page:

KaAbBa: The Great Pyramid is The Tree of Life: MerKaBa

Secrets Revealed in The MerAkhutu

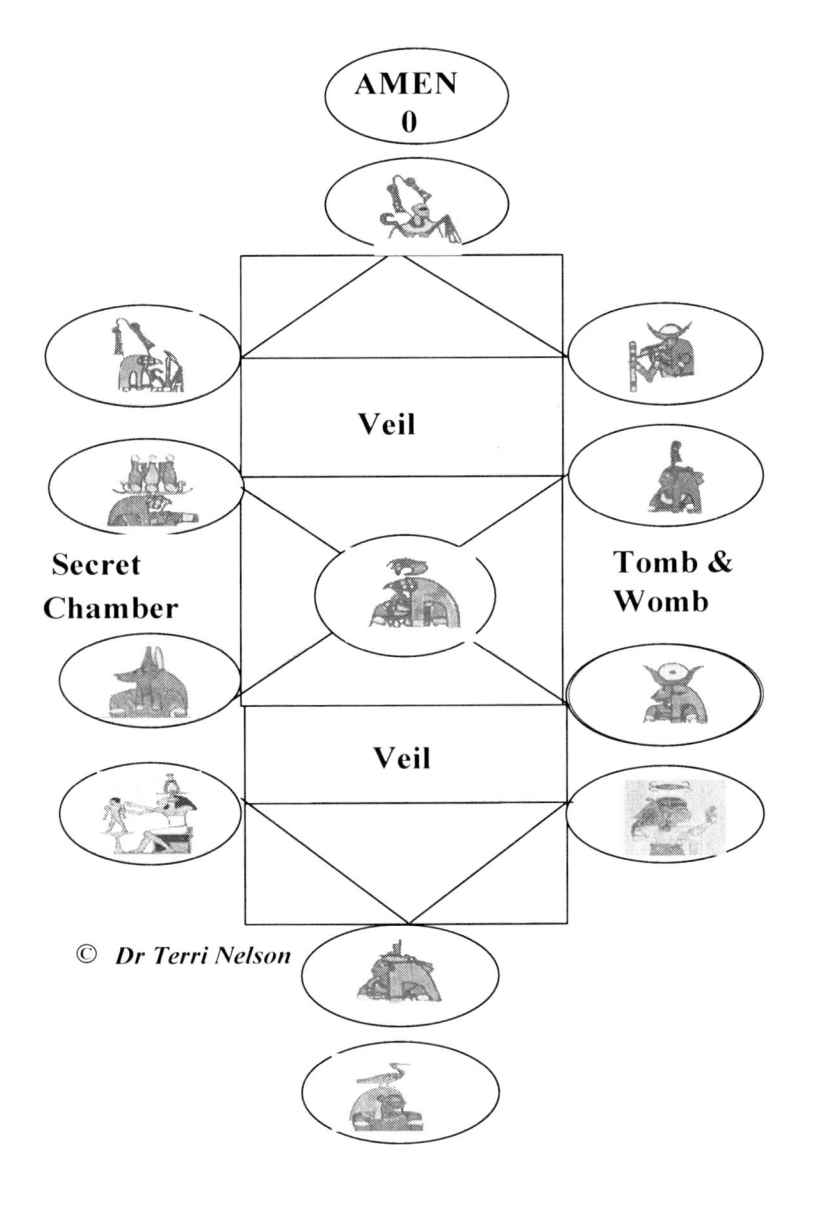

© Dr Terri Nelson

> Metaphysical Key in Consciousness:

▲ The 7 Planes of Consciousness

The 7 Planes of Consciousness are seen from two different angles within the MerKaBa in the diagrams on the next two pages:

Again the reader is urged to see, *Ka Ab Ba Building The Lighted Temple/The Metaphysical Keys to the Tree of Life,* for fuller explanation on the 7 Planes of Consciousness.

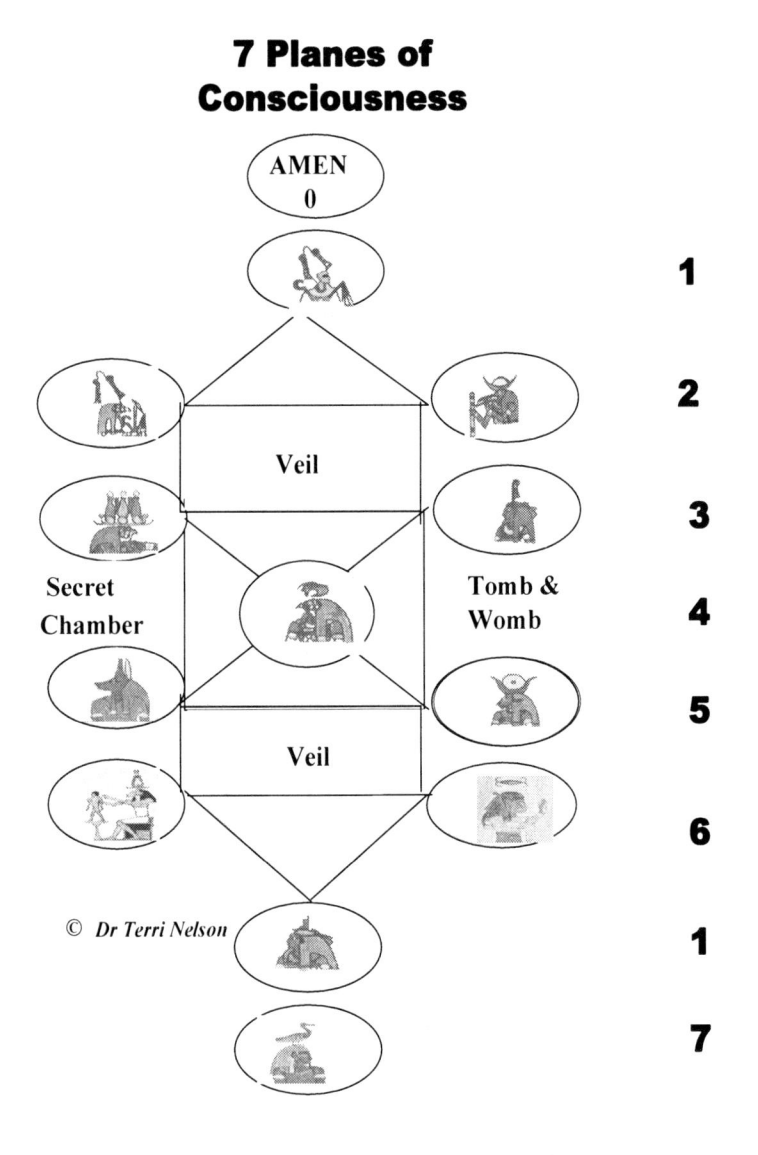

7 Planes of Consciousness

Neteru revealing Harvest to the Sons and Daughters of God

Tree of Life Great Pyramid MerAkhutu

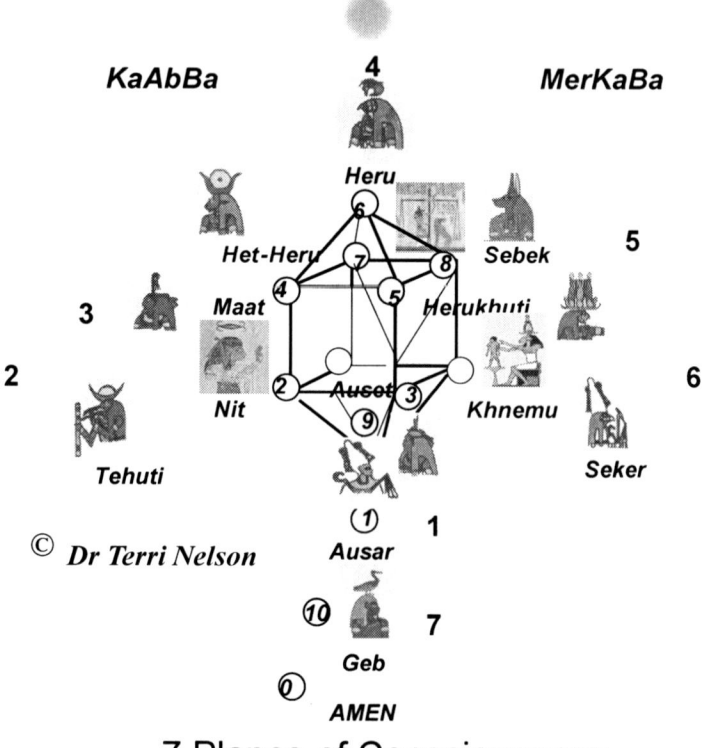

KaAbBa   **4**   MerKaBa

Heru

Het-Heru   Sebek   **5**

3   Maat   Herukhuti

2   Nit   **6**

Tehuti   Khnemu

Seker

© *Dr Terri Nelson*   Ausar   **1**

Geb   **7**

AMEN

7 Planes of Consciousness

> Metaphysical Key in Consciousness:

▲ The Djed/Tet Pillar

▲ Symbol of Stability

Again the reader is urged to see, *Ka Ab Ba Building The Lighted Temple/The Metaphysical Keys to the Tree of Life,* for fuller explanation on the 7 Planes of Consciousness and 7 Kemetic Soul Bodies. The Djed/Tet Pillar of Ausar, the symbol of stability is pictured on the following two pages:

> Metaphysical Key in Consciousness:

▲ Raising The Djed/Tet Pillar Tamarisk, Erika, Evergreen, Karest-mas, Christ-mas Tree - *to stand*

▲ The Ka-rest-mass/Christ-mas Tree

▲ 7 Soul Bodies of Kemetic Psychology/Spirituality

▲ Kemetically Conscious Ka-rest-mas

▲ Adorning/Decorating The Djed/Tet Pillar Tamarisk, Erika, Evergreen, Karest-mas, Christ-mas Tree with spheres of Light

We at last come to a crowning symbol, the Ka-rest /Christ-mas Tree which reveals embedded within, the 7 Soul Bodies of Kemetic Psychology/Spirituality and

Dr Nteri Nelson   *Nteri Renenet Elson*

Neteru revealing Harvest to the Sons and Daughters of God

The Djed/Tet Pillar pictured on the two pages that follow:

As we reclaim our ancient Afrikan wisdom from distortion and dispel the illusion, we can celebrate a Kemetically Conscious Ka-rest-mas as the Evergreen Tree is a symbol of our eternal life. When we raise the The Ka-rest-mass/Christ-mas Tree, Tamarisk, Erika, Evergreen, Karest-mas, with spheres of Light let us cause the symbol of stability the Djed/Tet Pillar of Ausar, to stand within us. Let us adorn it with the lighted Neteru bulbs, one for each of the spheres and Soul Bodies.

The Karest/Christ-mas Tree, the Djed/Djed/Tet Pillar of Ausar, the symbol of stability is pictured below:

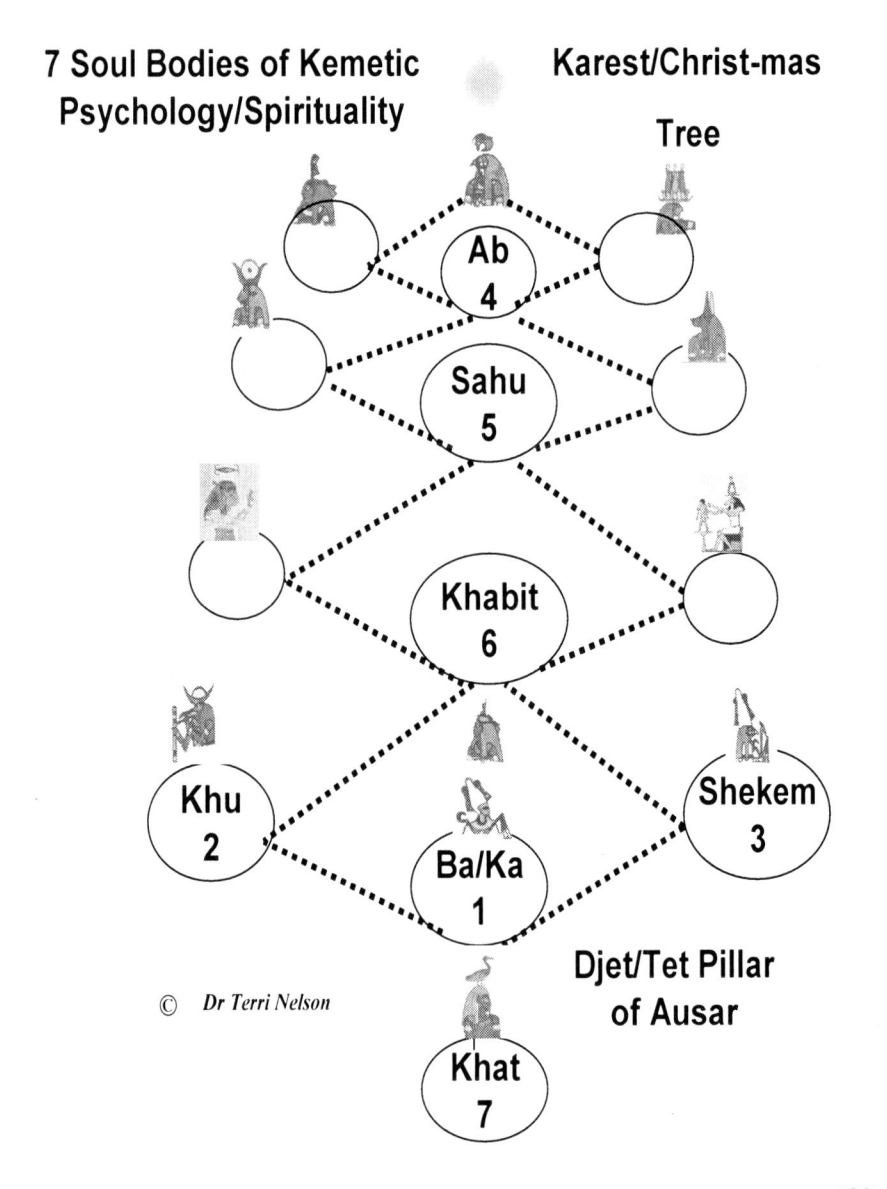

7 Soul Bodies of Kemetic Psychology/Spirituality

Karest/Christ-mas Tree

Ab 4

Sahu 5

Khabit 6

Khu 2

Ba/Ka 1

Shekem 3

Djet/Tet Pillar of Ausar

© *Dr Terri Nelson*

Khat 7

123

Within the KaAbBa: The Great Pyramid is The Tree of Life: MerKaBa Secrets Revealed in The MerAkhutu, the so-called hidden mysteries are 'encrypted'. But where is the crypt? In this Capstone book we have returned to the sarcophagus, the tomb of Khufu, an ancestor who has revealed much. Perhaps you have visited the granite tomb which is his crypt in the MerkaBa, Great Pyramid, MerAkhutu.

When you circumambulate around and around, run your fingers along the granite, see the much that may be revealed. These works represent both early eye opening and advanced studies as a Kemetician, Metaphysician, Kemetic Psychologist and Spiritualist.

Metaphysical Key in Consciousness:

▲ The MerKaBa Model

The 'linear' Tree of Life pictured may be cut out and folded to look like the MerKaBa. Cut out yours and begin meditation within. It should look like the one on the front book cover. This is pictured on page 128:

- We must bend over backwards to become anew
- *Anu* being as our Kemetic practice teaches
- We must bend over backwards such that head touches toes
- In the conscious union of Spirit and Matter
- Reuniting the Father and Mother –The Primal Couple within
- In perfect balance and equipoise
- Then the heart of the full blazing resurrected Sun – Son/Daughter stands revealed
- Dressed in the finest raiment from Head *to* Heart *to* Toe   Ba Ab Ka
- As the Diamond – no longer in the rough
- But the highly burnished gem
- The Lighted Temple
- *MerKaBa is Built*

The Great Pyramid *is*

The Tree of Life *is*

© Vladimir Melnik,.shutterstock.com

The Tree of Life *is*

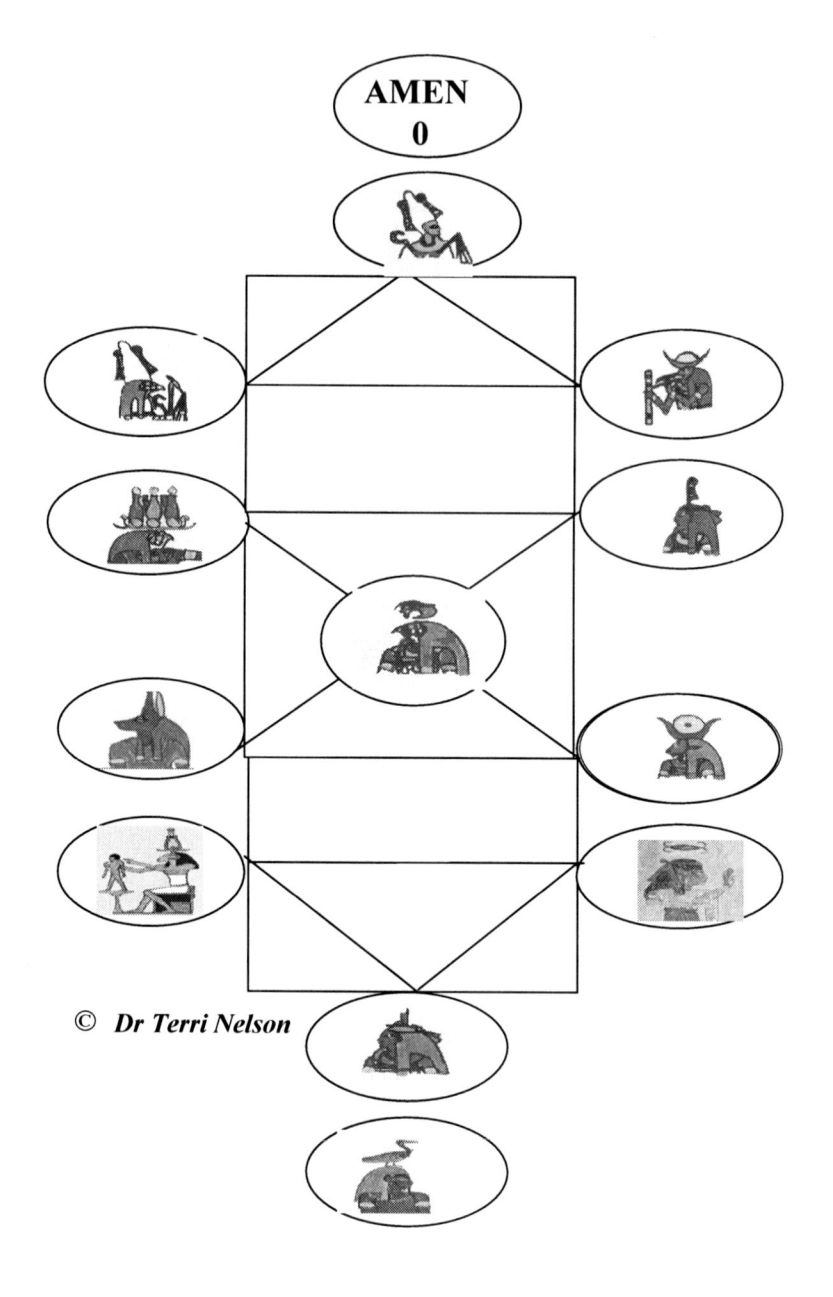

© *Dr Terri Nelson*

The MerKaBa

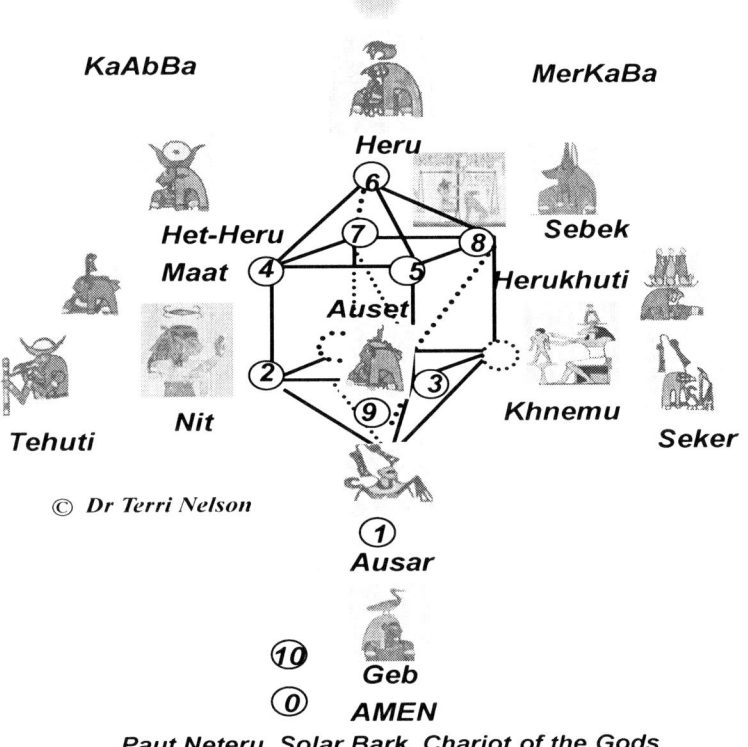

Tree of Life Great Pyramid MerAkhutu

KaAbBa

MerKaBa

Heru

Het-Heru
Maat

Sebek
Herukhuti

Auset

Tehuti

Nit

Khnemu

Seker

© *Dr Terri Nelson*

Ausar

Geb

AMEN

Paut Neteru, Solar Bark, Chariot of the Gods

Appendix

> Metaphysical Key in Consciousness:

Sacred Symbols, Demystifying, Decoding, Dis-spelling, Revealing, Unveiling, Unshrouding, Connecting The Dots, Activating the 1st Eye, Panoply Seen, Lineage Understood, Ungarbling the Garbled, Greatness Revealed, Neteru Livingness, Neteru Resurrection

Dr Terri Nelson aka Nteri Renenet Elson

Revealing the Harvest of the Neteru to the Sons and Daughters of God

Kemet Decoding Journal &Lecture Series
Afrikan Origins of The Ancient Wisdom

Taking It To The 'B'ONE

In order to tell a more completed story it is important to 'connect the dots'. The excerpts from the Journal Article/Lecture that follow present images along with the briefest of narrative and are intended to do just that, *connect the dots*. It is not intended to be an exhaustive Treatise on the Kemetic and Metaphysical meaning of these symbols nor their subsequent re-dispensation and packaging. The Journal Articles/Lecture Series are for this intended purpose as they present opportunity for the coming together of Group Mind, Consciousness, and 1st Eye to fully reveal and illuminate. This is copyrighted material and should be treated as such with full attribution to the author and author's ordering of images, selected quotes and original text to make intellectual and intuitive connections, reveal, and give insights, even without exhaustive elaboration.

Purpose of Lecture/Journal Article Series

●Empowerment through Knowledge

●Healing Deep Psychological Impacts

● Unpacking and Revealing Symbolic Meaning

●Attribution of the Afrikan Root Source Contribution

●Dis-spelling Illusion, Awakening, 1st Eye Restoration

●Acknowledging and Accrediting The Greatness of the Black Race

●Understanding Metu Neter's Journey into English
●Great-ness UnGarbled

●Understanding the Psychological & Spiritual Journey of Unfolding Consciousness

What Follows are Sample Excerpts From
Lecture/Journal: *Academy of Kemetic Education, Inc*.

See www.rrrk.net for information on the Journal/Lecture series

Title: *Ausar, The Pope, Santa Claus, Christmas, and Christianity*

By **Dr Terri Nelson aka Nteri Renenet Elson.**

Kemetician, Metaphysician, Practitioner, Wordsmith, Neteru Harvester/Revealer, Teacher, Healer, 1st Eye Activator

Ausar is the Supreme Neter of Kemet. He is pictured here seated upon his thrown in white mummy cloth and the white Atef crown.

Ausar

Hymn to Ausar

This Hymn to Ausar gives insight into the Afrikan reverence for this Supreme Neter. It is from the Prt M Hru, erroneously called the Egyptian Book of The Dead.

"Glory be to Ausar Un-nefer, the great god within Abtu (Abydos), King of eternity, Lord of the everlasting, who passeth through millions of years in his existence. Eldest son of the womb of Nut, engendered by Seb the Erpat, Lord of the crowns of the North and South, Lord of the lofty white crown. As Prince of gods and of men he hath received the crook and the flail and the dignity of his divine fathers. Let thy heart which is in the mountain of Amenta be content, for thy son Heru is stablished upon thy throne. Thou art crowned lord of Tattu (lower Kemet {Egypt]) and ruler in Abtu. Through thee the world waxeth green in triumph before the might of Neb-er-tcher (lord of eternity). He leadeth in his train that which is and that which is not yet, in his name Ta-her-set-nef (the one who draws the world); he toweth along the earth in triumph in his name Seker (Ptah, a form of the night sun). He is exceedingly mighty and most terrible in his name Ausar. He endureth for ever and for ever in his name Un-nefer (Good Being, Exalted Being). Homage to thee, King of kings, Lord of lords, Prince of princes, who from the womb of Nut hast possessed the world and hast ruled all land and Akert (Akert or AЖERT is the 'country' of which Ausar was prince). Thy body is of gold, thy head is of azure, and emerald light encircleth thee. O An (a name or form of Ra, the Sun-god) of millions of years, all-pervading with thy body and beautiful in countenance in Ta-sert (name of the underworld).

Symbols of Power

Scepter, Flail and Crook (shepherd's).

The Crown(s)

Here we see Ausar pictured below and holding the Scepter, Flail and Crook (shepherd's). On the next page we see pictured Pope Benedic XVI carrying the staff or scepter in his recent visit to the United Sates. Notice similarity of crown-headdress and official staff(s) in the next three pages. This Christian re-dispensation of God incarnate or God figure representative, on Earth, is from ancient Afrikan Spirituality, which predates it.

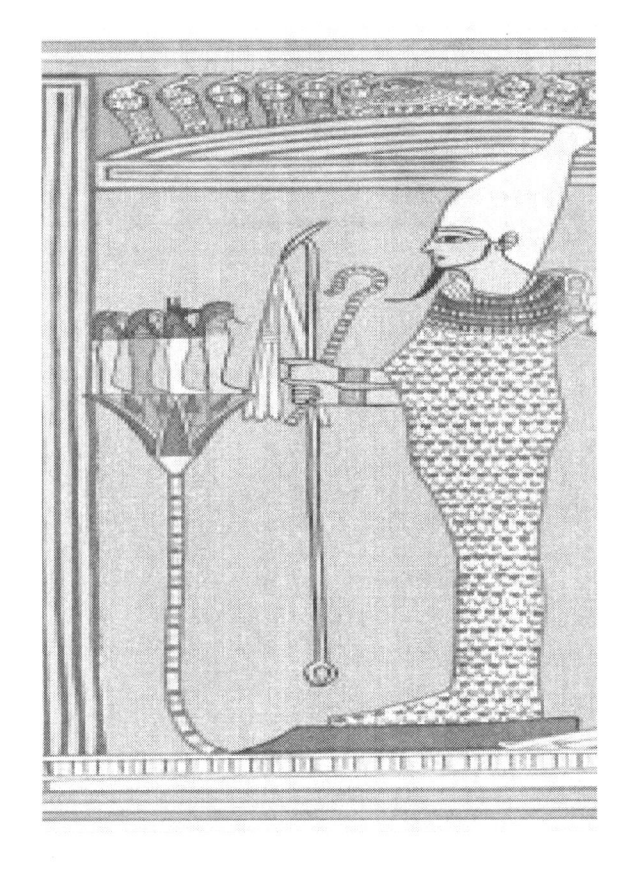

Dr Nteri Nelson   *Nteri Renenet Elson*

Neteru revealing Harvest to the Sons and Daughters of God

Pictured below is POPE JOHN XXIII. Notice again the crown headdress he is wearing and its similarity with the crown of Ausar. Pope John XXIII (reigned 1958-1963) is shown wearing the papal tiara, also called the *triregnum*

Hymn to Ausar

Crowns of the North and South

Let us more closely examine these words regarding the crowns from the Prt M Hru,

> "Glory be to Ausar Un-nefer, …lord of the crowns of the North and South, lord of the lofty white crown. Exalted Being. Homage to thee, King of kings, Lord of lords, Prince of princes…"

The Kemetic White and Red crown of Kemet becomes distorted into the Santa Claus Hat

The Pope in the Crown of the North and South

Notice the pope appearing in a red and white 'crown'. Festive coincidence or re-disensation?

The caption under his picture reads:

Pope Benedict XVI looked like he was getting into the festive spirit when he appeared at the Vatican wearing a Santa-style hat. The Pope appeared in St Peter's Square wearing a red cloak and a red velvet hat lined with white fur. Officials said the hat, known as a camauro, has been part of the papal wardrobe since the 12th century. It has not been worn in public since the death of John XXIII in 1963 reports BBC online.

Pope in 'Kemetic Crown of North and South'

It is important to have understanding of the psychological imprint of such images and their associative impacts. That the pope is wearing the traditional Santa Claus hat 'crown' at left. Notice that it is the same shape and color as the Kemetic Crowns of the North and South - the white and red crown – which, when combined stand for the unification of the two lands.

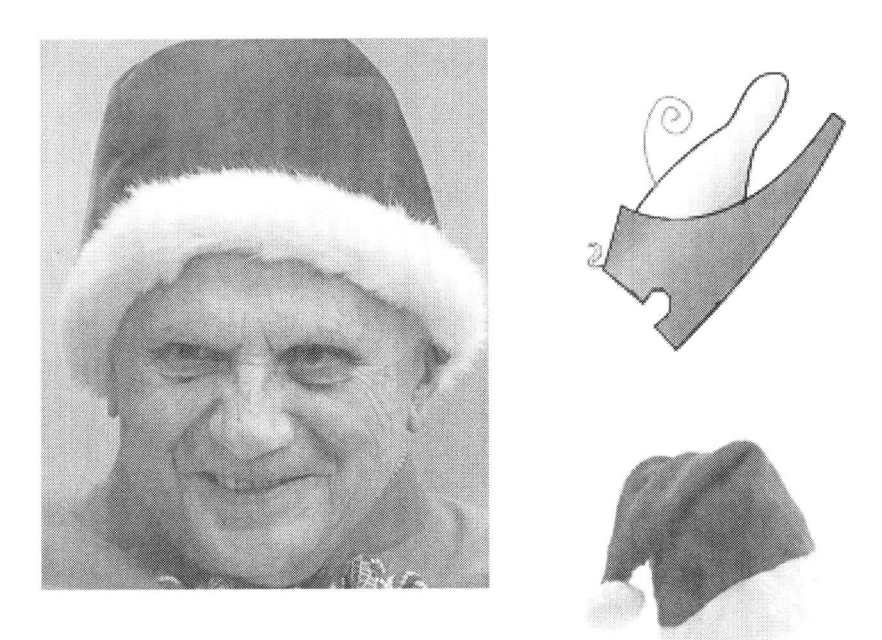

The Kemetic White and Red crown of Kemet becomes distorted into the Santa Claus Hat.

Crowned Son of Ausar - Heru

The picture on the next page is from the Judgment Scene of the Hall of Amenta. Ani, far left has just had his heart weighed upon the scales of Ma'at. He is being led by Heru, second from the left, who is wearing the double red and white crown. Heru is Isu the Karest, later called Jesus the Christ and the son of God by Christianity. Ausar is seated on his throne. Ani is brought by the son of God to come and kneel before 'The Awesome 'Presence', The Neter/Lord of The World and The Lord of Eternity, AUSAR (WSIR). We see here what would later be the biblical re-dispensation of, "Jesus saith unto him, I am the way, the truth, and the life. No one can come before the Father, except through me, the son" (John 14:6).

Sledge and Sleigh

Pictured above on the next page is the Ark of the Neter/God Seker, on its Sledge. The name given to the Seker Boat is Hennu. When we dis-pell this symbol we see its lineage in what would later become the 'Sleigh', pictured below. Notice the antlers in both pictures. The Sledge bears the Divine 'Presence' of Neter or Deity, the Sleigh bears Santa Claus with Christmas 'presents'. When we stand before Ausar, The Neter/Lord of the World, we want to be with/as and in receipt of the Awesome Presence and not in receipt of the material presents of Christmas.

The Sacred Boat

This Sacred Boat has profound meaning in Afrikan Spirituality as glimpsed in the following passage:

According to the Prt m Hru, p. 505.

"On the great day of the festival of Seker which was celebrated in many places throughout Kemet (Egypt), the ceremony of placing the Seker boat upon its sledge was performed at sunrise…The whole ceremony was under the direction of the high priest of Memphis…this official was expected to lift the Seker Boat upon its sledge, and to march at the head of the process of priest which drew the loaded sledge round the sanctuary. By this action the revolution of the sun and other celestial bodies was symbolized…"

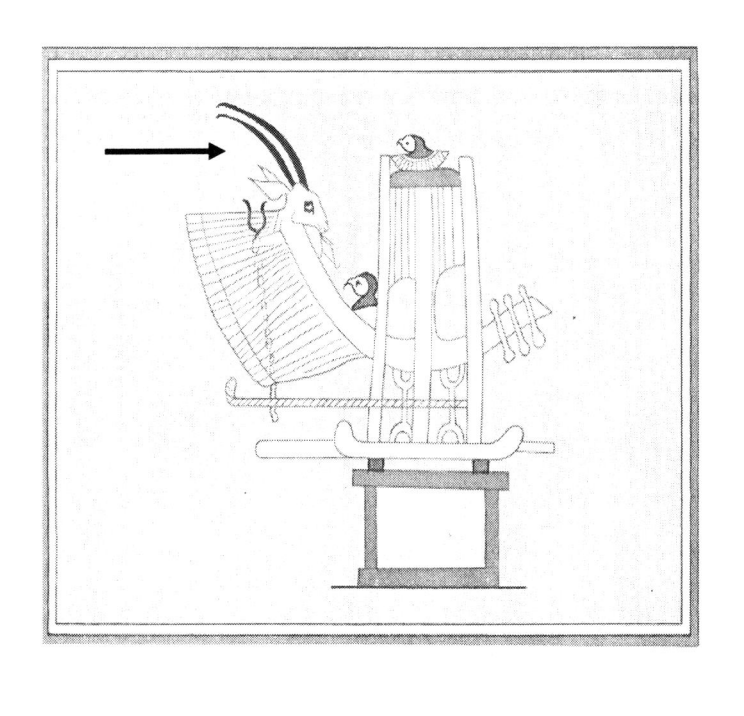

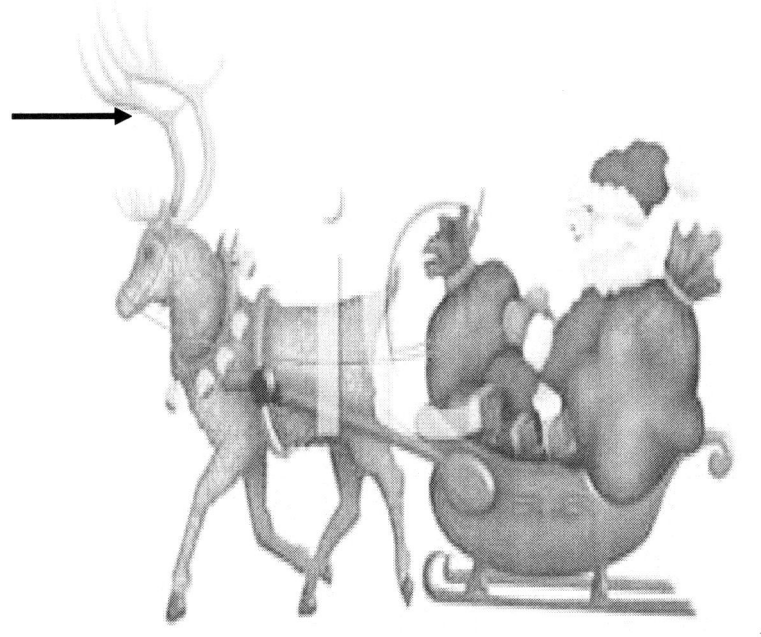

Neteru revealing Harvest to the Sons and Daughters of God

Afrikan Features

Here again we see the Kemetic Deity Ausar at right. Notice the strong Afrikan features and the beard.

Deity/Symbol Mockery

Notice how the Kemetic Deity here is imitated and made a caricature of Hollywood mockery.

Neteru revealing Harvest to the Sons and Daughters of God

Papal Coat of Arms and Smai Tawi Symbols

This symbol is the Coat of Arms of Pope Benedict XVl. picture below: A few things to notice are: 1.The crowned figure with prominent Afrikan features. Do you find this curious? 2. The crossed Keys behind the shield. 3. The 'tassled' rope that loops from the left side to the right side in essence joining or 'uniting' the two sides.

This is none other than a re-dispensation, albeit perversion, of the ancient Kemetic Smai Tawi Symbol pictured on the following page: Notice the same looping from the left side to the right side in essence joining or 'uniting' the two sides. The Smai Tawi symbol is a symbol of union. It is the Union of forces within ourselves.

It is the establishment of Unity vs. struggle, harmony vs discord. Here it is the lotus and papyrus plants that loop from one side to another. The lotus is the symbol of the South or white crown of Kemet, while the Papyrus is the Symbol of the North, the Red crown of Kemet. It is also the symbol of uniting the physical and the spiritual aspects with man and woman. Notice how the crowned Afrikan figure on the left and the bear on the right in the Papal symbol have replaced the Nile God Hapi on the left and on the right in the Smai Tawi symbol pictured on the following page:

KaAbBa: The Great Pyramid is The Tree of Life: MerKaBa
Secrets Revealed in The MerAkhutu

Neteru revealing Harvest to the Sons and Daughters of God

Here we see the symbol of unity with the Neteru Set on the left side and Heru on the right. Also the Neteru are shown in reverse order. Again, notice the 'tassel' in the looping of the lotus and papyrus plants from one side to another and the union of both Heru and Set pictured on the following page:

KaAbBa: The Great Pyramid is The Tree of Life: MerKaBa
Secrets Revealed in The MerAkhutu

Again, notice the Smai Tawi symbol is carved on the throne of the King of Kemet symbolizing the union of the North and the South and its distortion in relationship the Coat of Arms, both pictured on the following page:

KaAbBa: The Great Pyramid is The Tree of Life: MerKaBa
Secrets Revealed in The MerAkhutu

Khepera and Papal Coat of Arms Symbols
Kemetic Symbols Re-dispensation/Distortion

When we unpack this symbol more through our lecture series we see that it is a re-dispensation of Khepera, the symbol of the creation of Universe itself. (see, *Ka Ab Ba Buiding The Lighted Temple,* for more about the meaning of Khepera).

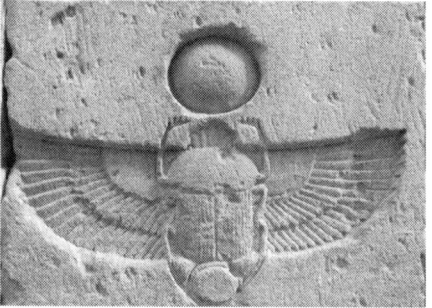

Above here we see Khepera and her dung ball containing her eggs. Notice Khepera in the symbol below.

Balance vs. Imbalance of Male and Female Energy

Notice in the picture above Ausar is seated on the throne with the balance of feminine energy at his side as represented by his wife, the Queen Auset, and their sister Nephthys (Het-Heru). Yet in the picture below Pope Benedict XVI is seated upon the throne with masculine energy on both his sides. One may only look around to behold what kind of world has been built when there is a shift in the presence of the feminine Neter and energy when, 'left out of the picture'. Let us ponder the deeply psychological work within the human family. Let us ask, can we even see clearly and completely the divinely intended design without the presence of the feminine?

KaAbBa: The Great Pyramid is The Tree of Life: MerKaBa
Secrets Revealed in The MerAkhutu

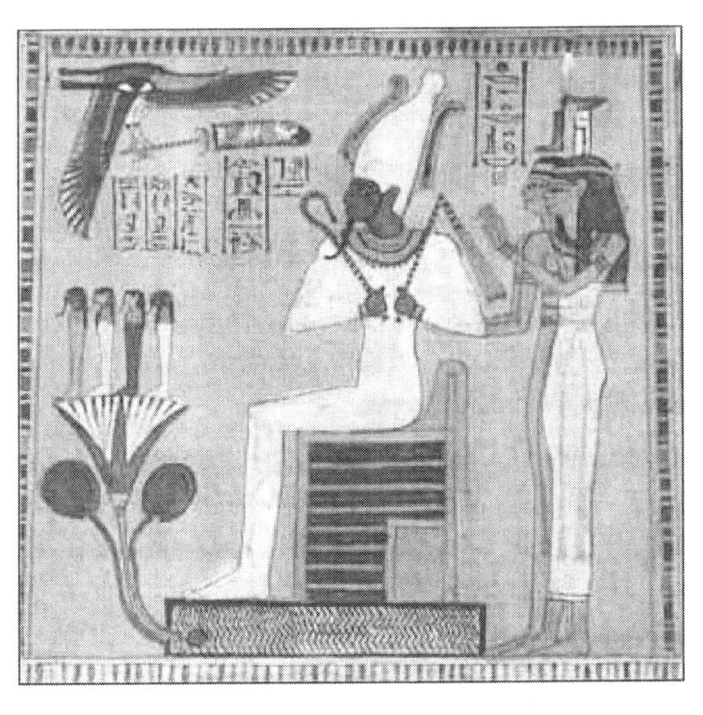

▲ Bibliography:

Nelson, Terri Nelson. (2000). *KaAbBa Building The Lighted Temple.* Mattapan, MA: Academy Kemetic Education.

Nelson,Terri Nelson. (2000).*Secrets of Race & Consciousness.* Mattapan, MA: Academy Kemetic Education.

Nelson, Terri Nelson. (2008). *Ausar, The Pope, Santa Claus, Christmas, and Christianity.* Mattapan, MA: Academy Kemetic Education.

(Nelson, Terri Nelson. (2009). *Afrikan Cosmology of Kemet The Golden Sun Egg Uncracked. The NU'N' Word Negg ur The Goose Goddess Who Laid The Sun Egg, the Cosmic Egg.* Mattapan, MA: Academy Kemetic Education.

Nelson, Terri Nelson. (1996). *On The Way To Finding Your Soulmate.* Mattapan, MA: Academy Kemetic Education.